UNCOLLECTED POEMS AND PROSE OF EDWIN ARLINGTON ROBINSON

ACKNOWLEDGMENTS

Permission to reprint "MacDowell's Legacy to Art" granted by the New York *Times;* "Plummer Street, Gardiner, Maine" by Harvard College Library and David S. Nivison; "Vachel Lindsay" by *Elementary English Review;* "Introductory Letter" to Christy MacKaye, *Wind in the Grass* by Harper & Row, Publishers, Inc.; "Ballade of Dead Mariners," "Doubts," "Tavern Songs: Chorus," "Antigone," "Edward Alphabet" from Denham Sutcliffe, editor, *Untriangulated Stars: Letters of Edwin Arlington Robinson to Harry DeForest Smith 1890-1905,* and two limericks from Richard Cary, editor, *Edwin Arlington Robinson's Letters to Edith Brower* by Harvard University Press; quotations from Rollo Walter Brown, *Next Door to a Poet* by Hawthorn Books, Inc.: quotations from Winfield Townley Scott. "To See Robinson" in the *New Mexico Quarterly,* XXVI, by Mrs. Winfield Townley Scott; "Perry, Thomas Sergeant" in *Dictionary of American Biography,* XIV, by Charles Scribner's Sons.

Permission to include such poems, essays, or brief comments for which there is no extant copyright holder authorized by David S. Nivison as executor and family representative.

UNCOLLECTED POEMS AND PROSE OF EDWIN ARLINGTON ROBINSON

Compiled and Edited,
with Introduction and Notes, by

RICHARD CARY

COLBY COLLEGE PRESS
Waterville, Maine

CONTENTS

POEMS

INTRODUCTION

In the fall of 1920 Edwin Arlington Robinson was walking across the Boston Common with William Stanley Braithwaite. As he tells it: "We passed the Park Street Church with its beautiful Wren steeple, and crossed onto the Mall, when I said to him, 'Robinson, don't you think it is time for a collected edition of your poems?' He threw up his head in amazement and said, 'Who would want a collected edition of my works?' " It turned out that a considerable number of readers and the Pulitzer Prize Committee — who chose it for the poetry award in 1922 — would want it. But Robinson's congenital reticence could not readily admit so grand a prospect.

Braithwaite persisted. Robinson should bring up the subject of a collected edition to his publisher. Again Robinson demurred.

> "Will you do it?" I insisted.
>
> "Well," he said, "there can be no harm in that." He dropped the matter there.
>
> That was in the fall. In March, I had a note from him which read something like this . . . : "Since you were crazy enough to suggest that I should have a collected edition of my verse, I think you ought to be the first to know. I've just come from Macmillan, and they have agreed to bring out the collected edition of my poems."[1]

The number and intensity of self-scarifying sessions Robinson endured before developing the grit to broach such a project can only be conjectured. Not that he lacked confidence of its worth. He was one of those votaries to perfectionism who, having scaled a peak, can never quite convince himself that he is there. The book, now definitely in the works, became for him a simulacrum of all he had suffered to incite it to life. He saw a touch of the monstrous in it, a psychic phenomenon not unlike Dr. Frankenstein's physical improvisation. "The collected works of E.A.R. — God help him — the paper of which in all probability he manufactured from the gray fibre of E.A.R.'s unhappy soul," he wrote Louis Ledoux.[2] And after the embodiment occurred he said dubitably, wistfully to Ridgely Torrence: "Your lyrical reception of my barge makes me hope that the thing may stay afloat, at least for a while. And even if it should become waterlogged, I still hope that a few planks and hen-coops may continue to get themselves washed ashore."[3]

In reviewing his nine books of published poems to decide which selections to jettison, Robinson seems to have undergone little hesitation and no agonies of filicide. When the contents were ready for the printer, he listed with remarkable composure fifteen pieces from *The Children of the Night* (1897) that were "sentenced to death": "The World," "Ballade of a Ship," "Two Octaves," "For Some Poems by Matthew Arnold," "Kosmos," "For a Book by Thomas Hardy," "The Miracle," "The Night Before," "Walt Whitman," "Romance [I. Boys; II, James Wetherell]," "Octaves I, III," and "Ballade of Dead Friends." "There are several more that ought to go," he added, "but I have decided to let them die a natural death."[4] He makes no mention here that he permanently excised the sestet from the sonnet "Boston."

Robinson first collected all the above in *The Torrent and The Night Before* (1896) and/or *The Children of the Night* in the following year. At the time he transferred the bulk of his first book to the second, he eliminated "For Calderon" and "A Poem for Max Nordau," which he never revived. From *The Children of the Night* he also dropped the title poem; from *The Town Down the River* (1910), "Normandy" and "Au Revoir"; from *Captain Craig* (1915), "With Sappho's Compliments," # V of "Variations of Greek Themes." He incorporated intact *The Man Against the Sky* (1916), *Merlin* (1917), *Lancelot* (1920), *The Three Taverns* (1920), and *Avon's Harvest* (1921) in *Collected Poems* (1921) and all his later books in sequent editions of the omnibook.

Robinson rarely specified why he debarred certain poems from the canon.[5] On the whole he was content to discharge them with generality: "when the pote himself doesn't like a thing, I suppose he can only act accordingly. Doubtless some one or other will cuss me for almost anything that was left out."[6] He knew from many recurrences of a morning when "I took the hyphen out of 'hell-hound'; and this afternoon I put it back,"[7] that writing poems was as much a matter of perspiration as of inspiration. Yet he also subscribed to the mystic concept that he builded better than he knew. "The only intelligent way to consider the artist is as an instrument played upon by something he does not understand."[8] It is therefore not surprising that he dodges positive statement. He countervailed the request of one editor for his personal opinion of his best poem with, "Possibly I am the last person to know."[9] At age 26 he stated unequivocally, "I cannot judge my own work at all."[10] Coupled with his assertion at age 60 that "No poet can be an adequate judge of his own writing,"[11] his sustained posture may be taken as bedrock honesty.

Poems

Collected in the first section of this volume are the twenty-two above-named poems; seventeen others Robinson published in newspapers, magazines, or books but never included in a volume of his own; and fifteen which first reached print in essays, biographies, and letters after his death. Of these fifty-four, three are translations from the Latin, one from the French; eight are fragments. "The Clam Digger: Capitol Island," buried in the pages of the *Kennebec Reporter Monthly* since April 1890, is here restored to the Robinson roster. Excluded is "Ballade of the Maine Law," which Hagedorn and Neff erroneously ascribed to Robinson.[12]

In the case of "Ben Jonson Entertains a Friend from Stratford" and "Nimmo's Eyes" (later "Nimmo"), both of which may be found in the *Collected Poems,* short portions are admitted to this volume because Robinson effaced them completely after original appearance in periodicals. Stanzas 2 and 3 of "The House on the Hill" are not accorded the same courtesy because Robinson replaced them with new ones. Thus they fall under the aegis of revision rather than dismissal. The same is true of "Horace to Leuconoë," extensively different in its collected version.[13] These, and others, are germane to a variorum rather than an uncollected edition. Robinson extirpated two stanzas from "Twilight Song" before submitting the poem for publication but they have been reinstituted by two perhaps overzealous academics. Robinson also deleted the fragment *Modred* before printing *Lancelot* but was compelled to issue it separately to protect himself from ravage by literary pirates.

The parturition and demise of Robinson's fugitive verses engender a chronicle worth assembling here for its insights into his creative divagations and for its value as increment to the bibliographic log.

Hermann Hagedorn and Laura E. Richards tell similar stories about Robinson's earliest known rejections of his "poetical effusions." He would read them aloud to friends around the furnace in the cellar of Gardiner High School. Then — whether approved or condemned — he would thrust the poems into the flames with some such remark as, "I don't think they amount to anything." Ergo, concludes Mrs. Richards, "we have no Juvenilia."[14] The lone survivor from these days is the opening tercet from a parody of Francis Mahony's "Shandon Bells," fortuitously recalled by one of Robinson's schoolmates:

> With deep affliction
> And malediction
> I often think of those Randolph bells,[15]

Randolph being the town across the Kennebec River from Gardiner.

The probability remains that Robinson's first publication, sometime during his high school period, was a versified conundrum. On page 79 of *The "Golden Days" Puzzlers' Directory* (Philadelphia, 1886), published by James Elverson, appears the entry: Robinson, E.A. (*"1812"*), Gardiner, Me. On page 140 it is cross-indexed: *1812*—E.A. Robinson, Gardiner, Me. *Golden Days for Boys and Girls,* a popular magazine which ran from 1880 to 1907, featured regularly a department of riddles and puzzles, many of them in meter and rhyme. Search through the relevant years of *Golden Days* by the present editor and by staff members of four university and public libraries has failed to turn up Robinson's assumptive contribution. It may be supposed that Robinson falls into the second group designated on the title page of the *Directory*: "Comprising nearly four thousand names and twelve hundred noms de plume of not only contributors to 'Golden Days,' but many other publications." Robinson's enigma will likely be exhumed one day by a serendipitous researcher.

At the high school graduation exercises on June 15, 1888 Robinson, dubbed class poet, read his poem "Mulieria, A Metrical Discourse." Next day the *Kennebec Reporter* described it as "humorous, witty and pleasing. It is to be hoped that his dream experience with 'woman' will never be realized in his waking hours. But it made the theme for a very entertaining discourse." On the 20th the Gardiner *Home Journal* called it "a masterpiece of thought, relating in verse the experience he underwent in a dream. It is rendered more interesting by the easy, off-hand manner in which he recited it." The longest account is by Hagedorn (pp. 44-45).

> The poem was called "Mulieria" and dealt satirically with the dangerous sex. There was a town, it seemed, which was inhabited only by women —
>
> "wherein could be seen
> Not one single pair of pantaloons."
>
> The poet tells how, impelled by curiosity, he makes his way into the town and is taken into custody by the petticoated policemen. A dangerous situation! What to do? He tries this device and that . . .
>
> "And then at last, still trusting to their natur'
> I thrust into their hands the last *Delineator*."
>
> That does the trick. The women start quarrelling over the fashion magazine, and in the general fracas, he escapes.

Here again, as with the unrecovered puzzle and the later "*Antigone*," loss is to be deplored. Hagedorn (p. 387) explains that "So far as the author could discover, Mr. Robinson's class poem survives only in the fragments quoted, as recalled by Mr. [Willis P.] Atwood." And Mrs. Richards (p. 29) further avows: "I have found no copy of this discourse."

While at Harvard in 1891-1893 Robinson toyed with and destroyed sheaves of poetical inklings. Some he revived in drastically altered form and published; others he dispatched beyond the realm of evidence. One line of one opuscule he favored long enough to preserve for his friend Harry Smith: "I have the idea of a ballade with a refrain, 'When Themes are due on Friday next.' If I ever work it out I may spring it on the *Lampoon*."[16] He may have worked out this Gallic confection and may in time have sprung it on the *Lampoon,* but it never metamorphosed into print.

Robinson's prolonged collaborative translation (with Smith) of Sophocles' *Antigone,* begun shortly after his departure from Harvard and still on his mind as late as 1897, is amply documented in the notes to that poem at the rear of this volume. It was a major project and a major disappointment to the evolving poet.

Robinson's undeserved image as an inveterate sobersides in his poetry (*vide* for one instance "Captain Craig") is effectively refuted by this Ogden Nashish jape at the start of a letter to Daniel Gregory Mason in winter 1900:

> Your confidential postal cards are always messengers of joy, and this last one is particularly reassuring. It tells me that your jokes are tuneful and that there are things in Boston to make you think of the vernal equinox. Here it is different, but even though cold retards
>
> The patient shards*
> In my back-yards,
> And postal-cards
> (With my 'regards'
> Are not for Bards
> Who flee towárds
>
> James Everard's on Twenty-Third Street for beer after improving and encouraging conversations with pleasant people . . .[17]

A one-line apostrophe to a pest constitutes another of Robinson's known abortive poems. Louis Untermeyer recalls an evening at the MacDowell Colony when a small group was discussing famous birds — Keats's nightingale, Shelley's skylark, Swinburne's swallow, Heine's seagull, Whitman's hermit-thrush, Poe's raven, and Frost's ovenbird. The question arose:

> "But who," said one of us, "will write the perfect poem about the whippoorwill?" They had been particularly persistent that summer.
> "I tried such a poem," said Robinson to everyone's surprise. "It began:
>
> *Thou iron-lunged incessant bird of Hell!*
>
> Then I had to stop. I found I had written the whole poem. That line said it all."[18]

A quarter-century later Untermeyer's memory attributed far larger eloquence to Robinson on that occasion:

"I started a poem a little while ago, but it wasn't meant to be a masterpiece, and I never got even as far as the second line. It was to be an ode to a bird — but an ode of hate to the local whippoorwill, the fiend whose inexhaustible energy keeps us all awake. The first line went like this:

Thou iron-lunged, incessant bird of Hell!

That's as far as I got. But it was far enough. I had written the poem. That line said it all."[19]

Prose

The second section of this volume comprises every known publication by Robinson in prose.

Robinson responded with "amazement" to the suggestion that his poems be collected. He would have been appalled, probably distraught, by any similar proposal in respect to his published prose. In the interval following Harvard Robinson applied himself unsparingly over a series of short stories which he planned for a volume to be called *Scattered Lives.* Later in the game he wrote two plays, then tried to convert them and at least one of his successful poems into novels. Regardless, in his heart he knew that this medium missed his message. "I may go back to poetry — which is always profitable and popular when compared with the kind of prose I seem destined to write," he told his cohort and patron Louis Ledoux.[20] Not a single effort of Robinson's in prose narrative fiction ever found its way into print. His compensation for such utter failure was to write his "dime novels" in verse, issuing a dozen of them in his last fifteen years.

He did, however, turn out twenty-six items that qualify for inclusion here. Fourteen may be classified as essays within the comprehensive reach of that term, the majority of them in the promotional mode (to adorn a cause or please a friend), or out-and-out hack jobs. The rest are a mismatched gallery of two obituaries, one book review, three introductions to books, one newspaper editorial, one biographical and four autobiographical sketches. Robinson spelled out his principle against book reviews to an editor for whom he had refused to appraise a new book by Thomas Hardy: "I am inclined to believe that the poetry-makers should stick to their trade and leave criticism to the others. I may change my mind, but that has been my attitude, in spite of a few lapses, for the past thirty years."[21] He manifestly counted among his "lapses" the three introductions and the several blurbs he permitted.

Four long excerpts from letters and an extended quotation from an interview are encompassed here because in each instance Robinson knew or could expect that his statements would be published. It is presumed that he informed these with as much circumspection as he did the essays.

The overriding characteristic of Robinson's prose is a singsong flatness. It suffers from an overplus of parallelism and replication, alliteration, euphemisms and tautologies which the wiles of rhyme and meter can disguise and make palatable. In view of these defects and Robinson's expressed distaste for his own prose, why collect at all? Not least, the bibliographic sanction: to make accessible to devotees and scholars under one convenient cover a conclusive record of Robinson's writings in this genre. Further, they contain valuable data on his life and his works, categorical or implied, from the poet's own slant and in his own words. Finally, they provide a fertile matrix for assessment of developing stages and ideas, opportunities for evocative analogies and analysis, footing for inferential meanings in his poems, and for angled scrutiny of his omnifaced psyche. Robinson was a dark, delicate, and sometimes devious sensibility. Nothing he wrote is not revelatory.

Briefs

The third section of this volume presents from more than sixty sources noteworthy comments made by Robinson and recorded by friends or interviewers. Some few are extracted from letters but, as above, only those to editors, anthologists, symposiarchs, scholars, solicitors of tributes, and lecturers of whose intent to publish Robinson was well aware. A substantial variety of his oral observations, epigrams and *obiter dicta* were caught by interlocutors and set down in critiques, memoirs, and biographies. Primarily, those touching on writing and writers are here renewed, with a modicum of others on persons and topics of sustaining interest. Interstitial punctuation and verbiage by the second party are deleted. Typographical errors are silently corrected.

Supererogatorily, Robinson bared his most visible trait to Walter Tittle: "I am rather shy myself"; and to Ridgely Torrence: "I was born with my skin inside out." The adjectives invoked by Untermeyer to depict him — shy, withdrawn, reticent, remote — are echoed in scores of portraits, notably Amy Lowell's. Robinson's scorn of self-advertisement, what he called "the luxuries of publicity," inspired the subtitles to Douglas Gilbert's article in the New York *Telegram* of January 3, 1931: NOT FOR MORGAN'S WEALTH WOULD HE READ HIS VERSE IN PUBLIC/GLAD AT RECOGNITION OF HIS WORK, BUT ESTEEMS HIS DETACHMENT MORE. When Karl Schriftgiesser pressed him for information about his "personal way of doing things," Robinson checked him curtly: "I don't care for this kind of interview." Schriftgiesser owlishly deduced that "Mr. Robinson hates to be interviewed. He is the shyest of men."

Two other journalists found thmselves facing the same implacable barricade. The persistent, thwarted, anonymous reporter for the Boston *Post* on May 30, 1913:

> About himself and his own poetry Mr. Robinson continually refused to talk in spite of repeated attempts to draw him into the subject. All through the interview he showed a great unwillingness to commit himself on any questions, and it was only with difficulty that a few scattered remarks were worked from him. What he did say he modestly insisted was of no real importance: "only a few haphazard thoughts."
>
> When questioned about himself and his work Mr. Robinson simply said: "I have nothing to say about myself. My poems speak for themselves . . ."

And the less perturbable Herbert S. Gorman in the New York *Sun* on January 4, 1920: "He never talks around a subject. When he is unwilling to express himself upon a topic he simply shuts his mouth and says nothing, while the interviewer — like a tiny balloon — floats debonairly on all by himself." As for the lucrative lecture circuit, Robinson said definitively: "For me a public platform would be nothing less than a public execution."[22]

Even situations unmarked by the menace of public exposure, in meetings arranged by amiable associates with confirmed admirers, Robinson could not step out from behind that thick asylum wall. During Lucius Beebe's undergraduate days at Harvard he induced Braithwaite to bring Robinson to his rooms for dinner.

> I anticipated a session of highly literary conversation, during which the Great Man would discuss matters of great poetic import, and with the brandy and cigars I settled down for what I naively hoped might be a sort of Mermaid Tavern evening with epigrams and much fine talk.
>
> But to my dismay, Robinson would say little enough on the subject of poetry and nothing of himself.[23]

On several occasions Robinson stoutly declared his reluctance to pass judgment on other writers, particularly contemporaries. "Who am I to do it?" he would ask.[24] Fortunately for literary history he overcame this disinclination with reasonable frequency and refreshing candor. After what was for Robinson a cheeky disquisition on the relative merits of Kipling, Housman, Amy Lowell, and Vachel Lindsay, Louis Untermeyer remarked: "It was one of the longest speeches I ever heard him make"[25] — a scant eighty-three words.

Notwithstanding Robinson's propensity for discreet silence, he did make a quantum of memorable remarks, cast in the shape of axiom or paradox, delivered in a tone of resignation or mild skepticism or droll self-detraction. The motives adduced above for collecting his longer prose apply as forcefully for these shorter, more widely disseminated utterances.

POEMS

THALIA

Morocco, and the Muse, and mimicry
Of what God never made and never meant
For man—Himself—diaphanously blent
With living shadows, play the mastery:
Pollio capers with Terpsichore,
While ass-eared Midas, swinishly content,
Wallows and roots amid the mire anent,
Nor peers beyond the spangled scenery.

We know not, dying, what we may be, dead;
We know not, living, what we are, alive:—
While painted Sorrow's mercenary laugh
Is linked with living lies, and ever read
As truth—throughout this humming human hive
Where is the man to write man's epitaph?

PALAEMON—DAMOETAS—MENALCAS

Menalcas.
Whose flock is that, Damoetas? Meliboeus'?

Damoetas.
No, Argon lately placed them in my care.

M.
O sheep! forever an unhappy flock!
While, fearful of my own supremacy,
Argon himself the fair Naera courts,
The guard Damoetas drains them twice an hour
And robs the lambs and mothers of their milk.

D.
Less freedom, sir, in dealing words to men;
For well we know both who corrupted you
And what the goats with sidelong glances saw;
And more, we know the cave wherein 'twas done—
The kindly Dryads laughing all the while.
("And the good-natured Nymphs etc.")

M.

And doubtless, too, they saw me with my knife
To cut the vines and tender shoots of Ulycon.

D.

Or rather when amidst this ancient wood
You broke the arrows and the bow of Daphne's
Which you, Menalcas, grieved to see returned
And would have died but for the pain you gave him.

M.

Where are the masters while their raging slaves
Dare to address me thus! O wicked one,
Did I not see you trap the goat of Damon,
Lycisca barking madly all the time?
And when I called out, "Tityrus, where goes he?
Collect your flock!"—you hid among the sedge.

D.

And should he not yield up the goat to me,
Since with my voice and reed I conquered him?
If you would know it, sir, the goat is mine:
Damon himself confessed as much to me,
Yet says he cannot pay one what is due.

M.

You won a prize at singing! as if you
Could play a waxen reed! Why clown, 'tis yours
To blow your murderous note upon the highway.

D.

Lo! shall we have a contest here between us?
I'll take this heifer, and, lest you refuse
I'll say she comes to milking twice a day,
And feeds two calves besides. Now, my good friend,
What pawn will you advance to cover mine?

M.

I dare not meet thy wager from the flock:
My father is at home, and worse than that,
A crabbed step-dame: both count twice a day
The sheep, and one the kids. But I will pledge—
Since 'tis your will to carry out this folly—

What you yourself will own far worthier:
These beechen cups wrought for Alcimedon
On which the ivy, exquisitely carved
With facile chisel, sweetly intermingles
Its scattered fruit and pallid foliage.
Two figures are engravéd in the center:
The one is Conon, and—who was the other?—
Who with his rod marks out the world for man—
The time for ploughing and for harvesting?
These are kept hidden; lips have never touched them.

D.

Alcimedon has made for me two bowls
And wound the handles round with acanthus;
With Orpheus graven in a woodland scene.
These two are hidden; lips have never touched them.
Yet if you will but look upon my heifer
The cups are nothing to deserve your praise.

M.

Let there be no delay, for I will come
Wherever you may call. Or let the one
Who now approaches hear us—look—Palaemon.
And I will take good care that in the future
Damoetas tortures no man with his voice.

D.

Begin, if you have anything to sing;
You'll find me ready, nor will I dispute
The judgment; therefore, my good friend Palaemon,
This contest; 'tis no trifling affair.

Palaemon

Sing, as we sit amid the tufted grass:
Now all the field and all the wood is blooming;
The trees are green, the year is in its glory,
Begin, Damoetas, and Menalcas follow;
Alternately—the way the muses love.

D.

Begin with Jove, O Ulysses! all things are full of Jove:
'Tis he that loves the earth; 'tis he that loves my song.

M.
Phoebus loves me; for him I ever keep close by
His chosen gifts; the laurel and blushing hyacinth.

D.
Galatea, playful maiden, seeks me with an apple;
Then flies, but wishes to be seen before she hides.

M.
My flame Amyntas comes of his own will to me,
And Delia to my dogs is now no better known.

D.
I'll make my love a gift: for I have found the spot
Where the high-soaring pigeons rear their tender young.

M.
I've sent my love ten apples all ruddy from the woodland—
As many as I could: I'll send ten more tomorrow.

D.
How many and how sweet the words of Galatea!
Bear them aloft ye winds, so may th'immortals hear them.

M.
Where is my joy, although you hold me dear, Amyntas,
While you pursue the goats for me to tend the toils?

D.
Bid Phyllis come to me, Iolas; 'tis my birthday.
I offer sacrifices ere long; then you may come.

M.
But I love Phyllis more: she weeps at separation;
And cries "Farewell! Farewell! a long farewell!"—Iolas.

D.
Wolves to the flock are fatal; showers to ripened grain;
Wind to the trees; to me the wrath of Amaryllis.

M.
Rain cheers the crops; arbutus is sweet to tender kids;
Osier to laden sheep, to me none save Amyntas.

D.

Great Pollis loves to hear the rustic song I sing;
O, mountain Muses, rear a heifer to your lover.

M.

He writes a wondrous song—Oh, feed the bull that now
Lifts high his head and spurns the sand beneath his feet.

D.

Who loves thee, Pollis, may win they cherished fame:
For him may honey flow and bramble bear amomum.

M.

Who hates not Bavius must love thy song, O Maevius!
And he would milk a butting goat, or yoke his foxes.

D.

O boys, who gather flowers and growing fruits of earth,
Flee hence!—a long cold snake is lying in the grass.

M.

My sheep, go not too near! you cannot trust the bank;
For even now the rain shakes out his dripping fleece.

D.

O Tityrus, from the stream call back your feeding flock:
Ere long I'll wash them all myself, in yonder spring.

M.

O boys, collect the sheep—if summer's burning heat,
As formerly, destroys the milk we work in vain.

D.

Alas! how lank and lean my bull stands in the field!
The love that kills the herd will kill the keeper too.

M.

But love is not in mine—their bones scarce held together:
I cannot tell the eye that charms my tender lambs.

D.

Oh, tell me in what land, and be my great Apollo,
Only three ells of sky lie open to the sight.

M.

Oh, tell me in what land the written names of kings
Are born with blooming flowers and Phyllis shall be thine.

Pal.

'Tis not for me to judge so fine a matter;
The prize belongs to one as to the other:
To any one who sings of love so sweet,
Or labors through such sorrow.—Now, my boys,
The rivers close—the fields have drunk their fill.

THE CLAM-DIGGER

CAPITOL ISLAND

There is a garden in a shallow cove
    Planted by Neptune centuries ago,
    Which Ocean covers with a thin, flat flow,
Then falling, leaves the sun to gleam above
Those oozy lives (which reasoning mortals love)
    Reposed in slimy silence far below
    The shell-strewn desert, while their virtues grow,
And over them the doughty diggers rove.

Then awful in his boots the King appears,
    With facile fork and basket at his side;
Straight for the watery bound the master steers,
    Where giant holes lie scattered far and wide;
And plays the devil with his bubbling dears
    All through the bounteous, ottoitic tide.

ISAAC PITMAN

With many a whirling dash of dim design
    He snares the flying thought in frenzy flung;
    The captive cadence of the human tongue
Follows his hand, immured in every line:

His labor through the centuries will shine,
And when this old man dwells no more among
The living, where his glories long have rung,
Calling his fellows to the phonic shrine —

Still will he walk Fame's flowering avenues,
Amid rich gardens through his life-work sown —
Fairer than vineyards in far Sicily;
And here the Master, mutely musing, views
New flowers springing where the old have grown,
The princely pageant of posterity.

THE GALLEY RACE

[AENEID] BOOK V, 104-285

The welcome day arrives; the rising sun
Brings the ninth morning in with glorious light
And all the neighboring country is aroused
By the great name and glory of Acestes.
An eager multitude they crowd the shore,
Some to behold the Trojans, some prepared
To enter for the glories of the day.
First, in their midst, the prizes are displayed;
The sacred tripods, wreaths of green, and palms;
Talents of gold and silver, arms and robes
Dyed with rich purple; now the trumpet's peal
Proclaims the joyous festival begun.
Four galleys chosen from the fleet appear,
Oared heavily and equally equipped.
The flying Pristis Mnestheus drives along
With rapid oars — Mnestheus of Italy
Soon after — whence have sprung the Memmii;
And Gyas with the great Chimera comes —
A huge affair, a city in itself —
Which Trojans in a triple line impel;
Sergestus (whence the Sergian house) commands
The mighty Centaur; and Cloanthus (whence

Your race Cluentius) the dark blue Scylla.
At sea, far distant from the foaming shore,
There is a rock, which when the wintry winds
Obscure the stars, is thumped and overwashed
By tumid floods; but when the waves are still
It rises silent from the silent sea,
A gracious haunt for sunny comorants [*sic*].
Here as a goal the great Aeneas fixed
A leafy oak, a signal for the seamen
That they may know the turning of the course.
Then lots are drawn for places, and the masters
Glitter in gold and purple from the sterns.
The crews are crowned with poplar leaves, and glossed
With oil, their naked shoulders turn the sun.
They take their seats and grasp with eager arms
The oars and anxiously await the sign,
While throbbing fears and burning hopes of praise
Glow in their ardent bosoms. Then at length,
When the clear trumpet sounds, without delay
All forge ahead, their clamor fills the air;
Torn by their arms the waters froth and foam;
Their wakes are equal and their trident beaks
Mixed with the oars tear up the foaming flood.
No flying chariot sweeps the field like these,
No charioteer so pays the loosened rein,
Nor hangs himself ahead to swing the lash.
Then all the grove resounds with shouts of men
And zealous cheers; along the curling shore
The voices roll; the quivering hills around
Throw back the clamor. Mid wild shoutings then
Leaps Gyas headlong, foremost in the fray;
Then comes Cloanthus, with more practiced oar,
But the huge weight of ship holds back itself;
Close after these the Centaur and the Pristis
Vie with each other striving for the lead:
'Tis now the Pristis, now the Centaur holds it;
Now they are borne together beak to beak,
Their long keels furrowing the salt sea waves.
Soon they approach the rock and reach the goal,

When conquering Gyas to the pilot cries,
"Why to the right! — come nearer — hug the shore!
So we may brush the rocks upon the left
Without the oars — let others hold away!"
He spoke, but blind Menoetes fearing reefs
Steered for the open sea. "Why thus Menortes [*sic*]!
Bear to the rock!" again called Gyas madly.
And now behold he sees Cloanthus coming
Close in the rear, to take the inner course;
Sheer to the left, between the sounding rocks
And Gyas' ship, he shoots a sudden course
And safely holds the sea beyond the goal.
Then fired with deep chagrin while tears of wrath
Rolled down his cheek, unmindful of the scene
And all regardless of the common safety,
He flung the dull Menoetes from the stern
Head-foremost to the sea, and took his post;
And mid the cheering of the sailors turned
The rudder to the rock. Now old Menoetes,
At length emerging from the water, climbs —
His heavy garments dripping in the sea —
High on the rock and perches in the sun.
The Trojans greet his tumble with a howl
And jeer him swimming; and they laugh aloud
To mark him heave and spew the swallowed brine.
Then to the minds of Mnestheus and Sergestus
A brave hope springs that they may overtake
The tardy Gyas. Now Sergestus leads
A little, and Pristis' forging beak
Comes tearing alongside. Then rushing down
Among the crew the urging Mnestheus cries:
"Now! friends of Hector, now! bend to the oars!
Ye comrades whom I chose from falling Troy
Now show that strength and zeal by which ye passed
Graetulian [*sic*] quicksands and Ionian seas!
Not that I hope to win the first reward —
(Ah, if I could!) — But let thy will prevail,
O Neptune! Shameful 'tis to be last —
Conquer it, friends! and save us from disgrace." —
Then all their power is given to the work;

The tall ship trembles with the giant strokes;
Drawing the sea beneath; with rapid breath
And parching throats their limbs are trembling,
And gushing sweat rolls over them in rivers.
Mere chance it was that gave the cherished glory:
Sergestus, furious, now turn'd his prow
Too near the rock and struck the jutting reef;
The rough crags trembled and the oars were snapped,
The broken beak hung pendant from the ledge;
The rowers with a might clamor cease
And rising seize sharp iron pikes and poles
And gather from the sea the broken oars.
But Mnestheus, joyful all the more for this,
With flying oars makes for the settling waves
And shoreward rushes down the spreading sea.
Just as a dove, whose home and cherished young
Lie in a rocky shade: the cave disturbed
And frightened from her nest she seeks the fields
With flapping wings, there through the tranquil air
She cuts a liquid course in silent flight.
So Mnestheus, so the Pristis cleaves the wave
Around the goal, borne by the impetus.
And now he leaves Sergestus on the rock
In shallow seas and vainly calling aid,
Striving to free his ship with shattered oars.
Soon the Chimera, Gyas' bulky craft —
The pilot gone — he overtakes and passes.
Cloanthus leading forges on ahead,
His only rival, whom he now pursues
With all his powers. Then great shouts arise
And all applaud while redoubled cheers
Roll through the trembling air. The Scylla's crew,
Scorning the thought of losing what is theirs,
Would willingly resign their lives for glory.
Success inflames the others: they can win
For they believe they can. Perchance they might
Have borne the prizes with an equal course
Had not Cloanthus, stretching out his hands,
Sought aid in prayers and called the gods to witness:
"Ye gods, who rule the sea, whose realms I sweep,

Joyfully will I offer unto you
Before the altar, on these shores, a bull
Snow white; and I will give unto the sea
His entrails, and pour out the flowing wine."
He spoke, and from the bottom of the deep
His voice was heard alike by all the Nymphs,
And Phorcus and the virgin Panopea,
While old Portunus pushed with mighty hands.
Swift as the wind in arrowy flight she speeds,
And rides triumphant in the land-locked port.
Then all are summoned while the great Aeneas
Declares Cloanthus victor in the race
And crowns his temples with a wreath of laurel.
Three bullocks are awarded to the ships,
And wine, together with a weight of silver.
The leaders he rewards with special honors:
A golden chlamys to the conqueror,
Bordered by waving Meliboean purple;
And there inwoven the boy Ganymede
Through Ida's grove pursues the weary deer,
Breathless yet eager in the pictured scene:
Him Jupiter's swift eagle has caught up
And borne away from Ida in his claws;
In vain the aged guards uplift their palms,
While howls of raging dogs wail through the air.
To Mnestheus next, who by his valor won
The second place, he gives a coat of mail
Jointed with hooks and triple wove of gold.
The prince had stripped it from Demoleos
Where rapid Simois flows by lofty Troy.
This he presents. A rich defence in war,
With difficulty two attendants bore
The ponderous folds away upon their shoulders;
Demoleos however, thus arrayed,
Pursued the straggling Trojans in their flight.
Two brazen caldrons Gyas then receives,
With richly figured drinking cups of silver.
At length, now all rewarded and rejoicing,
They issue forth their temples bound with purple,
When, from the fateful rock released, Sergestus

Paddled with scanty oars his crippled craft,
Scoffed and unhonored. As a snake, o'ertaken
Upon the highway, which a wheel has crossed
Or traveller with heavy blow has struck
And left half-dead and ground beneath a rock,
Vainly retreating, curls its tortuous length
And hissing rears its head with glittering eyes,
Ferocious; though retarded by the wound
Twisting and writhing struggles on its way,
So the slow ship worked inward to the shore;
Now sails are set, and thus with spreading sheets
She enters port. Aeneas, gratified
To see the ship restored with all its crew,
Allows the foiled commander as a prize
Pholoe, a Cretan slave with nestling twins.

TRIOLET

Silent they stand against the wall,
The mouldering boots of other days.
No more they answer Duty's call —
Silent they stand against the wall, —
Over their tops the cold bugs crawl
Like distant herds o'er darkened ways.
Silent they stand against the wall.
The mouldering boots of other days.

BALLADE OF A SHIP

Down by the flash of the restless water
The dim White Ship like a white bird lay;
Laughing at life and the world they sought her,
And out she swung to the silvering bay.
Then off they flew on their roystering way,
And the keen moon fired the light foam flying
Up from the flood where the faint stars play,
And the bones of the brave in the wave are lying.

'Twas a king's fair son with a king's fair daughter,
And full three hundred beside, they say, —
Revelling on for the lone, cold slaughter
So soon to seize them and hide them for aye;
But they danced and they drank and their souls grew gay,
Nor ever they knew of a ghoul's eye spying
Their splendor a flickering phantom to stray
Where the bones of the brave in the wave are lying.

Through the mist of a drunken dream they brought her
(This wild white bird) for the sea-fiend's prey:
The pitiless reef in his hard clutch caught her,
And hurled her down where the dead men stay.
A torturing silence of wan dismay —
Shrieks and curses of mad souls dying —
Then down they sank to slumber and sway
Where the bones of the brave in the wave are lying.

ENVOY

Prince, do you sleep to the sound alway
Of the mournful surge and the sea-birds' crying? —
Or does love still shudder and steel still slay,
Where the bones of the brave in the wave are lying?

IN HARVARD 5

In Harvard 5 the deathless lore
That haunts old Avon's classic shore
Wakens the long triumphant strain
Of Pride and Passion, Mirth and Pain,
That fed the Poet's mind of yore.

Time's magic glass is turned once more
And back the sands of ages pour,
While shades of mouldered monarchs reign
In Harvard 5.

Thin spirits flutter through the door,
Quaint phantoms flit across the floor:
  Now Fancy marks the crimson stain
  Of Murder. . . . and there falls again
The fateful gloom of Elsinore.

In Harvard 5.

MENOETES

Who is this fellow floundering in the wave,
  Flung from the Trojan galley thundering by?
  Lightly, my friend; he may be you, or I!
This passage from the master to the slave
Is but a flash; the pinnacle we crave
  Totters and falls; and life is but to fly
  The dark immediate anguish surging nigh —
To foil the shrewd enclosure of the grave.

So, when I read of old Menoetes thrown
  By raging Gyas to the furrowed brine,
I cannot wholly laugh: there is a tone
  Of merry sadness in the poet's line
  That tells me summer suns will never shine
When skies with tyrannous clouds are overblown.

BALLADE OF DEAD MARINERS: ENVOI

Days follow days till years and years are fled;
Years follow years till hopes and cares are dead,
And life's hard billows boom their message home:
Love is the strongest where no words are said,
And women wait for ships that never come.

DOUBTS

Yes, this is the end of life, I suppose —
    To do what we can for ourselves and others;
But men who find tragedy writ in a rose
    May forget sometimes there are sons and mothers —

Fathers and daughters of love and hate,
    Scattered like hell-spawn down from Heaven,
To teach mankind to struggle and wait
    Till life be over and death forgiven.

FOR A COPY OF POE'S POEMS

Like a wild stranger out of wizard-land
    He dwelt a little with us, and withdrew;
    Bleak and unblossomed were the ways he knew,
Dark was the glass through which his fine eye scanned
Life's hard perplexities; and frail his hand,
    Groping in utter night for pleasure's clue.
    These wonder-songs, fantastically few,
He left us. . . . but we cannot understand.

Lone voices calling for a dimmed ideal
    Mix with the varied music of the years
        And take their place with sorrows gone before:
Some are wide yearnings ringing with a real
    And royal hopelessness, some are thin tears.
        Some are ghosts of dreams, and one — Lenore.

THE MIRACLE

"Dear brother, dearest friend, when I am dead,
And you shall see no more this face of mine,
Let nothing but red roses be the sign
Of the white life I lost for him," she said;

"No, do not curse him, — pity him instead;
Forgive him! — forgive me! . . God's anodyne
For human hate is pity; and the wine
That makes men wise, forgiveness. I have read
Love's message in love's murder, and I die."
And so they laid her just where she would lie, —
Under red roses. Red they bloomed and fell;
But when flushed autumn and the snows went by,
And spring came, — lo, from every bud's green shell
Burst a white blossom. — Can love reason why?

TAVERN SONGS: CHORUS

There's a town down the river
Down the river, down the river,
There's a town down the river,
By the sea.

THE *ANTIGONE* OF SOPHOCLES

[1] "Your pleasure — of the friend as of the foe —
Is one with mine, O Creon."

[Lines 211-212
September 29, 1894]

[2] Nothing is there more marvelous than man!
Driven by southern storms he sails amidst
The wild white water of the wintry sea,
And through the thunder of engulfing waves;
And Earth — unceasing monarch of the gods —
He furrows, and the plows go back and forth,
And turn the broken mold year after year.

He traps and captures — all inventive man! —
The light birds and the creatures of the wild,
And in his nets the fishes of the sea;
He trains the tenants of the fields and hills,
And brings beneath the neck-encircling yoke
The rough-maned horse and the wild mountain bull.

[Lines 332-352
October 28, 1894]

[3] "— money is the most accursed thing
That man has ever made; it strikes down cities
And scatters families; it leads away
Good souls of men to foul accomplishments
And teaches them the practice of all guile
And all iniquity."

[Lines 296-301
November 4, 1894]

[4] Strophe II

Unsatisfactory

[And language has he learned and wind-swift thought]
And speech and soaring wisdom has he learned,
With human measures and a way to shun
The sharp and painful arrows of the frost.
Full of resource, of all the future brings,
Resourceless meets he nothing; Death alone
He never shall escape; but he has found
[A cure] for life's unyielding maladies. [a cure].

This is the part that sticks me more than all the rest.

Antistrophe II

Unsatisfactory

Thus gifted with a shrewd inventive skill
Beyond belief, now makes he for the right,
Now for the wrong. And first of all the state
Is he who honors most the nation's law
And the sworn justice of the gods; but he
Becomes an outcast whom rash folly binds
In evil fellowship, nor shall he dwell
With me, nor think with me, whose action
thus . . . .

I marvel at this portent of the gods!
Knowing her as I do can I deny
The maid Antigone? — O wretched girl —
Child of a wretched father, Œdipus,
Tell me! — they surely cannot lead you here
Captured in this wild work against the king!

The Ox breaks this line—you do not. I like it better broken, but can easily change it. How do the anchorites agree upon it? Perhaps this will go.

[Lines 354-383
November 4, 1894]

GUARD

Here is the guilty one that buried him —
We seized her in the work. — But where is Creon?

CHORUS

Returning from the palace — in good time
To meet your opportunity.

CREON

What is this?
I come to meet whose opportunity?

GUARD

O King, 'tis not for any man to say
What things he will not do; for second thoughts
Belie the first resolve. I could have sworn
That I should never come this way again
But slowly, for your threats; yet am I here
(For joy without our expectation
Has none to match it) spite of my past vow,
Leading this maiden whom we found at work
Over the dead man's grave. No shaken lot
Is this, but still my own good fortune — mine,
And only mine. — And now, O King, I pray you,
Take her and question her, and do with her
According to your will. But I am free,
And justly clear of this unhappy crime.

CREON

'Tis she you bring! and how? Whence do you
bring her.

GUARD

She buried Polynices; you know all
There is to know.

CREON

Is this the truth you tell me?

GUARD

I saw this maiden burying the corpse
Against your order. Do I speak straight words?

CREON

And how was she discovered? and how taken?

GUARD

'Twas thus: In terror of your fearful threat,
As soon as we were there we swept away
The dust that hid the corpse; and having stripped
The body, damp with death, we placed ourselves
High on a windward hill to shun the stench;
And there we waited, busily alert
With hard reproach for any man of us

Who made a sign to shirk. So the time passed
Until the noonday sun stood overhead,
Burning us with his heat — when suddenly
There came an awful whirlwind out of heaven
That filled the plain and all the mighty air
And vexed the woodland with unwholesome dust.
This god-sent plague we suffered with closed eyes;
And when it ceased, after a weary time,
We saw this maiden coming; and she cried
With a quick bitter wailing, like a bird
Over an empty nest. So grieved she then,
When she beheld the body lying bare,
And called down imprecations upon those
Who wrought the deed; and straightway did she bring
Dry dust in her own hands, and from an urn,
Well shaped of brass and lifted high in air,
Thrice did she crown him with poured offerings.
When we saw this we rushed at once upon her
And seized her, unappalled at our approach;
And when we there accused her of this crime
And of the first as well, she made no sign,
Nor uttered any word in her defense.
At once a pleasure and a pain to me
Was this: for, though it be a pleasant thing
To make one's own way out of jeopardy,
Painful it is to send another there.
But then all this was naturally less
To me than my own safety.

CREON (To Antigone)

Tell me, you
With your head bowed to earth, if you confess
Or you deny that you have done this thing.

ANTIGONE

Yes, I confess. [*Mss. note*] *It would hardly be kindness to Sophocles to reproduce an Attic redundancy in a language that won't stand it.*

CREON (To Guard)

You may go where you will,
Acquitted of this heavy charge. — (To Antigone)
But you
Will tell me, and that briefly, did you know
The proclamation that made this forbidden?

ANTIGONE

I knew it, and why not — 'Twas very plain.

CREON

And you have dared then to transgress the laws!

ANTIGONE

Yes, for the word was not of Jove at all;
Nor was it Justice, dwelling with the gods
Below the earth, that framed your government;
Nor did I think this edict you proclaimed
So strong that I could break the laws of heaven,
Unwritten and unchanging. For, O King,
They are not of today, nor yesterday,
But for all time they are, and no man knows
Of their beginning. It was not for fear
Of any human will that I would pay
The gods my penalty — for I must die.
Well did I know that ere I ever heard
Your proclamation; and if I die now,
Before my time, so much I count my gain:
For whosoever lives as I have lived,
In many sorrows, will by dying reap
His best reward. Therefore to meet my fate
The pain is nothing; but if I had left
The child of my own mother to lie dead
Without a mound above him — that indeed
Were sorrow; but there is no sorrow now.
And if by chance you still declare
What I have done to be a foolish thing,
Then I am charged with folly by a fool.

[Lines 384-470
November 11, 1894]

KOSMOS

Ah, — shuddering men that falter and shrink so
To look on death, — what were the days we live,
Where life is half a struggle to forgive,
But for the love that finds us when we go?
Is God a jester? Does he laugh and throw
Poor branded wretches here to sweat and strive
For some vague end that never shall arrive?
And is He not yet weary of the show?

Think of it, all ye millions that have planned,
And only planned, the largess of hard youth!
Think of it, all ye builders on the sand,
Whose works are down? — Is love so small, forsooth?
Be brave! To-morrow you will understand
The doubt, the pain, the triumph, and the Truth!

FOR A BOOK BY THOMAS HARDY

With searching feet, through dark circuitous ways,
I plunged and stumbled; round me, far and near,
Quaint hordes of eyeless phantoms did appear,
Twisting and turning in a bootless chase, —
When, like an exile given by God's grace
To feel once more a human atmosphere,
I caught the world's first murmur, large and clear,
Flung from a singing river's endless race.

Then, through a magic twilight from below,
I heard its grand sad song as in a dream:
Life's wild infinity of mirth and woe
It sang me; and, with many a changing gleam,
Across the music of its onward flow
I saw the cottage lights of Wessex beam.

EDWARD ALPHABET

Look at Edward Alphabet
Going home to pray!
Drunk as he can ever get,
And on the Sabbath day! —

THE CHILDREN OF THE NIGHT

For those that never know the light,
The darkness is a sullen thing;
And they, the Children of the Night,
Seem lost in Fortune's winnowing.

But some are strong and some are weak, —
And there's the story. House and home
Are shut from countless hearts that seek
World-refuge that will never come.

And if there be no other life,
And if there be no other chance
To weigh their sorrow and their strife
Than in the scales of circumstance,

'T were better, ere the sun go down
Upon the first day we embark,
In life's imbittered sea to drown,
Than sail forever in the dark.

But if there be a soul on earth
So blinded with its own misuse
Of man's revealed, incessant worth,
Or worn with anguish, that it views

No light but for a mortal eye,
No rest but of a mortal sleep,
No God but in a prophet's lie,
No faith for "honest doubt" to keep;

If there be nothing, good or bad,
    But chaos for a soul to trust, —
God counts it for a soul gone mad,
    And if God be God, He is just.

And if God be God, He is Love;
    And though the Dawn be still so dim,
It shows us we have played enough
    With creeds that make a fiend of Him.

There is one creed, and only one,
    That glorifies God's excellence;
So cherish, that His will be done,
    The common creed of common sense.

It is the crimson, not the gray,
    That charms the twilight of all time;
It is the promise of the day
    That makes the starry sky sublime;

It is the faith within the fear
    That holds us to the life we curse; —
So let us in ourselves revere
    The Self which is the Universe!

Let us, the Children of the Night,
    Put off the cloak that hides the scar!
Let us be Children of the Light,
    And tell the ages what we are!

"I MAKE NO MEASURE OF THE WORDS THEY SAY"

I make no measure of the words they say
Whose tongues would so mellifluously tell
With prescient zeal what I shall find in hell
When all my roving whims have had their day, —
I take no pleasure of the time they stay

Who wring my wasted minutes from the well
Of cool forgetfulness wherein they dwell
Contented there to slumber on alway; —

But when some rare old master, with an eye
Lit with a living sunset, takes me home
To his long-tutored consciousness, there springs
Into my soul a warm serenity
Of hope that I may know, in years to come,
The true magnificence of better things.

BOSTON

[*Following the octave*]

I know my Boston is a counterfeit, —
A frameless imitation, all bereft
Of living nearness, noise, and common speech;
But I am glad for every glimpse of it, —
And there it is, plain as a name that's left
In letters by warm hands I cannot reach.

FOR SOME POEMS BY MATTHEW ARNOLD

Sweeping the chords of Hellas with firm hand,
He wakes lost echoes from song's classic shore,
And brings their crystal cadence back once more
To touch the clouds and sorrows of a land
Where God's truth, cramped and fettered with a band
Of iron creeds, he cheers with golden lore
Of heroes and the men that long before
Wrought the romance of ages yet unscanned.

Still does a cry through sad Valhalla go
For Balder, pierced with Lok's unhappy spray —
For Balder, all but apared by Frea's charms;
And still does art's imperial vista show,
On the hushed sands of Oxus, far away,
Young Sohrab dying in his father's arms.

BALLADE OF DEAD FRIENDS

As we the withered ferns
    By the roadway lying,
Time, the jester, spurns
    All our prayers and prying —
    All our tears and sighing,
Sorrow, change, and woe —
    All our where-and-whying
For friends that come and go.

Life awakes and burns,
    Age and death defying,
Till at last it learns
    All but Love is dying;
    Love's the trade we're plying,
God has willed it so;
    Shrouds are what we're buying
For friends that come and go.

Man forever yearns
    For the thing that's flying.
Everywhere he turns,
    Men to dust are drying, —
    Dust that wanders, eying
(With eyes that hardly glow)
    New faces, dimly spying
For friends that come and go.

ENVOY

And thus we all are nighing
    The truth we fear to know:
Death will end our crying
    For friends that come and go.

FOR CALDERON

And now, my brother, it is time
For me to tell the truth to you:
To tell the story of a crime
As black as Mona's eyes were blue. —
Yes, here to-night, before I die,
I'll speak the words that burn in me;
And you may send them, bye-and-bye,
To Calderon across the sea.

Now get some paper and a pen,
And sit right here, beside my bed.
Write every word I say, and then —
And then . . . well, what then? — I'll be dead! —
. . . But here I am alive enough,
And I remember all I've done . . .
God knows what I was thinking of! —
But send it home — to Calderon.

And you, Francisco, brother, say, —
What is there for a man like me? —
I tell you God sounds far away —
As far — almost as far — as she!
I killed her! . . . Yes, I poisoned her —
So slowly that she never knew . . .
Francisco, — I'm a murderer. —
Now tell me what there is to do!

To die — of course; but after that,
I wonder if I live again!
And if I live again, for what? —
To suffer? . . . Bah! — there is no pain
But one; and that I know so well
That I can shame the devil's eyes! . . .
For twenty years I've heard in hell
What Mona sings in Paradise!

Strange, that a little Northern girl
Should love my brother Calderon,
And set my brain so in a whirl
That I was mad till she was gone! . . .

I wonder if all men be such
As I? — I wonder what love is! —
I never loved her very much
Until I saw that she was his; —

And then I knew that I was lost:
And then — I knew that I was mad. —
I reasoned what it all would cost,
But that was nothing. — I was glad
To feel myself so foul a thing! —
And I was glad for Calderon. . . .
My God! if he could hear her sing
Just once, as I do! — There! she's done. . . .

No, it was only something wrong
A minute — something in my head. —
God, no! — she'll never stop that song
As long as I'm alive or dead!
As long as I am here or there,
She'll sing to me, a murderer! —
Well, I suppose the gods are fair. . . .
I killed her . . . yes, I poisoned her!

But you, Francisco, — you are young; —
So take my hand and hear me, now: —
There are no lies upon your tongue,
There is no guilt upon your brow. —
But there is blood upon your name? —
And blood, you say, will rust the steel
That strikes for honor or for shame? . . .
Francisco, it is fear you feel! —

And such a miserable fear
That you, my boy, will call it pride; —
But you will grope from year to year
Until as last the clouds divide,
And all at once you meet the truth,
And curse yourself, with helpless rage,
For something you have lost with youth
And found again, too late, with age.

The truth, my brother, is just this: —
Your title here is nothing more
Or less than what your courage is:
The man must put himself before
The name, and once the master stay
Forever — or forever fall. —
Good-bye! — Remember what I say . . .
Good-bye; — Good-bye! . . . And that was all.

The lips were still: the man was dead. —
Francisco, with a weird surprise,
Stood like a stranger by the bed,
And there were no tears in his eyes.
But in his heart there was a grief
Too strong for human tears to free, —
And in his hand a written leaf
For Calderon across the sea.

THE WORLD

Some are the brothers of all humankind,
And own them, whatsoever their estate;
And some, for sorrow and self-scorn, are blind
With enmity for man's unguarded fate.

For some there is a music all day long
Like flutes in Paradise, they are so glad;
And there is hell's eternal under-song
Of curses and the cries of men gone mad.

Some say the Scheme with love stands luminous,
Some say 'twere better back to chaos hurled;
And so 'tis what we are that makes for us
The measure and the meaning of the world.

WALT WHITMAN

The master-songs are ended, and the man
That sang them is a name. And so is God

A name; and so is love, and life, and death,
And everything. But we, who are too blind
To read what we have written, or what faith
Has written for us, do not understand:
We only blink and wonder.

Last night it was the song that was the man,
But now it is the man that is the song.
We do not hear him very much to-day:
His piercing and eternal cadence rings
Too pure for us — too powerfully pure,
Too lovingly triumphant, and too large;
But there are some that hear him, and they know
That he shall sing to-morrow for all men,
And that all time shall listen.

The master-songs are ended? Rather say
No songs are ended that are ever sung,
And that no names are dead names. When we write
Men's letters on proud marble or on sand,
We write them there forever.

A POEM FOR MAX NORDAU

Dun shades quiver down the lone long fallow,
And the scared night shudders at the brown owl's cry;
The bleak reeds rattle as the winds whirl by,
And frayed leaves flutter through the clumped shrubs callow.

Chill dews clinging on the low cold mallow
Make a steel-keen shimmer where the spent stems lie;
Dun shades quiver down the lone long fallow,
And the scared night shudders at the brown owl's cry.

Pale stars peering through the clouds' curled shallow
Make a thin still flicker in a foul round sky;
Black damp shadows through the hushed air fly;
The lewd gloom wakens to a moon-sad sallow,
Dun shades quiver down the lone long fallow.

THE NIGHT BEFORE

Look you, Dominie; look you, and listen!
Look in my face, first; search every line there;
Mark every feature, — chin, lips, and forehead!
Look in my eyes, and tell me the lesson
You read there; measure my nose, and tell me
Where I am wanting! A man's nose, Dominie,
Is often the cast of his inward spirit;
So mark mine well. But why do you smile so?
Pity, or what? Is it written all over,
This face of mine, with a brute's confession?
Nothing but sin there? nothing but hell-scars?
Or is it because there is something better —
A glimmer of good, maybe — or a shadow
Of something that's followed me down from childhood —
Followed me all these years and kept me,
Spite of my slips and sins and follies,
Spite of my last red sin, my murder, —
Just out of hell? Yes? something of that kind?
And you smile for that? You're a good man, Dominie,
The one good man in the world who knows me, —
My one good friend in a world that mocks me,
Here in this hard stone cage. But I leave it
To-morrow. To-morrow! My God! am I crying?
Are these things tears? Tears? What! am I frightened?
I, who swore I should go to the scaffold
With big strong steps, and — No more. I thank you,
But no — I am all right now! No! — listen!
I am here to be hanged; to be hanged to-morrow
At six o'clock, when the sun is rising.
And why am I here? Not a soul can tell you
But this poor shivering thing before you,
This fluttering wreck of the man God made him,
For God knows what wild reason. Hear me,
And learn from my lips the truth of my story.
There's nothing strange in what I shall tell you,
Nothing mysterious, nothing unearthly, —
But damnably human, — and you shall hear it.
Not one of those little black lawyers had guessed it;

The judge, with his big bald head, never knew it;
And the jury (God rest their poor souls!) never dreamed it.
Once there were three in the world who could tell it;
Now there are two. There'll be two to-morrow, —
You, my friend, and — But there's the story: —

When I was a boy the world was heaven.
I never knew then that the men and the women
Who petted and called me a brave big fellow
Were ever less happy than I; but wisdom —
Which comes with the years, you know — soon showed me
The secret of all my glittering childhood,
The broken key to the fairies' castle
That held my life in the fresh, glad season
When I was the king of the earth. Then slowly —
And yet so swiftly! — there came the knowledge
That the marvellous life I had lived was my life;
That the glorious world I had loved was my world;
And that every man, and every woman,
And every child was a different being,
Wrought with a different heat, and fired
With passions born of a single spirit;
That the pleasure I felt was not their pleasure,
Nor my sorrow — a kind of nameless pity
For something, I knew not what — their sorrow.
And thus was I taught my first hard lesson, —
The lesson we suffer the most in learning:
That a happy man is a man forgetful
Of all the torturing ills around him.
When or where I first met the woman
I cherished and made my wife, no matter.
Enough to say that I found her and kept her
Here in my heart with as pure a devotion
As ever Christ felt for his brothers. Forgive me
For naming His name in your patient presence;
But I feel my words, and the truth I utter
Is God's own truth. I loved that woman, —
Not for her face, but for something fairer,
Something diviner, I thought, than beauty:
I loved the spirit — the human something

That seemed to chime with my own condition,
And make soul-music when we were together;
And we were never apart, from the moment
My eyes flashed into her eyes the message
That swept itself in a quivering answer
Back through my strange lost being. My pulses
Leapt with an aching speed; and the measure
Of this great world grew small and smaller,
Till it seemed the sky and the land and the ocean
Closed at last in a mist all golden
Around us two. And we stood for a season
Like gods outflung from chaos, dreaming
That we were the king and the queen of the fire
That reddened the clouds of love that held us
Blind to the new world soon to be ours —
Ours to seize and sway. The passion
Of that great love was a nameless passion,
Bright as the blaze of the sun at noonday,
Wild as the flames of hell; but, mark you,
Never a whit less pure for its fervor.
The baseness in me (for I was human)
Burned like a worm, and perished; and nothing
Was left me then but a soul that mingled
Itself with hers, and swayed and shuddered
In fearful triumph. When I consider
That helpless love and the cursed folly
That wrecked my life for the sake of a woman
Who broke with a laugh the chains of her marriage
(Whatever the word may mean), I wonder
If all the woe was her sin, or whether
The chains themselves were enough to lead her
In love's despite to break them. . . . Sinners
And saints — I say — are rocked in the cradle,
But never are known till the will within them
Speaks in its own good time. So I foster
Even to-night for the woman who wronged me,
Nothing of hate, nor of love, but a feeling
Of still regret; for the man — But hear me,
And judge for yourself: —

For a time the seasons
Changed and passed in a sweet succession
That seemed to me like an endless music:
Life was a rolling psalm, and the choirs
Of God were glad for our love. I fancied
All this, and more than I dare to tell you
To-night, — yes, more than I dare to remember;
And then — well, the music stopped. There are moments
In all men's lives when it stops, I fancy, —
Or seems to stop, — till it comes to cheer them
Again with a larger sound. The curtain
Of life just then is lifted a little
To give to their sight new joys — new sorrows —
Or nothing at all, sometimes. I was watching
The slow, sweet scenes of a golden picture,
Flushed and alive with a long delusion
That made the murmur of home, when I shuddered
And felt like a knife that awful silence
That comes when the music goes — forever.
The truth came over my life like a darkness
Over a forest where one man wanders,
Worse than alone. For a time I staggered
And stumbled on with a weak persistence
After the phantom of hope that darted
And dodged like a frightened thing before me,
To quit me at last, and vanish. Nothing
Was left me then but the curse of living
And bearing through all my days the fever
And thirst of a poisoned love. Were I stronger,
Or weaker, perhaps my scorn had saved me,
Given me strength to crush my sorrow
With hate for her and the world that praised her —
To have left her, then and there — to have conquered
That old false life with a new and a wiser, —
Such things are easy in words. You listen,
And frown, I suppose, that I never mention
That beautiful word, *forgive!* — I forgave her
First of all; and I praised kind Heaven
That I was a brave, clean man to do it;
And then I tried to forget. Forgiveness!

What does it mean when the one forgiven
Shivers and weeps and clings and kisses
The credulous fool that holds her, and tells him
A thousand things of a good man's mercy,
And then slips off with a laugh and plunges
Back to the sin she has quit for a season,
To tell him that hell and the world are better
For her than a prophet's heaven? Believe me,
The love that dies ere its flames are wasted
In search of an alien soul is better,
Better by far than the lonely passion
That burns back into the heart and feeds it.
For I loved her still, and the more she mocked me, —
Fooled with her endless pleading promise
Of future faith, — the more I believed her
The penitent thing she seemed; and the stronger
Her choking arms and her small hot kisses
Bound me and burned my brain to pity,
The more she grew to the heavenly creature
That brightened the life I had lost forever.
The truth was gone somehow for the moment;
The curtain fell for a time; and I fancied
We were again like gods together,
Loving again with the old glad rapture.
But scenes like these, too often repeated,
Failed at last, and her guile was wasted.
I made an end of her shrewd caresses
And told her a few straight words. She took them
Full at their worth — and the farce was over.

. . . . . .

At first my dreams of the past upheld me,
But they were a short support: the present
Pushed them away, and I fell. The mission
Of life (whatever it was) was blasted;
My game was lost. And I met the winner
Of that foul deal as a sick slave gathers
His painful strength at the sight of his master;
And when he was past I cursed him, fearful
Of that strange chance which makes us mighty
Or mean, or both. I cursed him and hated

The stones he pressed with his heel; I followed
His easy march with a backward envy,
And cursed myself for the beast within me.
But pride is the master of love, and the vision
Of those old days grew faint and fainter:
The counterfeit wife my mercy sheltered
Was nothing now but a woman, — a woman
Out of my way and out of my nature.
My battle with blinded love was over,
My battle with aching pride beginning.
If I was the loser at first, I wonder
If I am the winner now! . . . I doubt it.
My life is a losing game; and to-morrow —
To-morrow! — Christ! did I say to-morrow? . . .
Is your brandy good for death? . . . There, — listen: —

When loves goes out, and a man is driven
To shun mankind for the scars that make him
A joke for all chattering tongues, he carries
A double burden. The woes I suffered
After that hard betrayal made me
Pity, at first, all breathing creatures
On this bewildered earth. I studied
Their faces and made for myself the story
Of all their scattered lives. Like brothers
And sisters they seemed to me then; and I nourished
A stranger friendship wrought in my fancy
Between those people and me. But somehow,
As time went on, there came queer glances
Out of their eyes, and the shame that stung me
Harassed my pride with a crazed impression
That every face in the surging city
Was turned to me; and I saw sly whispers,
Now and then, as I walked and wearied
My wasted life twice over in bearing
With all my sorrow the sorrows of others, —
Till I found myself their fool. Then I trembled, —
A poor scared thing, — and their prying faces
Told me the ghastly truth: they were laughing
At me and my fate. My God, I could feel it —

That laughter! And then the children caught it;
And I, like a struck dog, crept and listened.
And then when I met the man who had weakened
A woman's love to his own desire,
It seemed to me that all hell were laughing
In fiendish concert! I was their victim —
And his, and hate's. And there was the struggle!
As long as the earth we tread holds something
A tortured heart can love, the meaning
Of life is not wholly blurred; but after
The last loved thing in the world has left us,
We know the triumph of hate. The glory
Of good goes out forever; the beacon
Of sin is the light that leads us downward —
Down to the fiery end. The road runs
Right through hell; and the souls that follow
The cursed ways where its windings lead them
Suffer enough, I say, to merit
All grace that a God can give. — The fashion
Of our belief is to lift all beings
Born for a life that knows no struggle
In sin's tight snares to eternal glory —
All apart from the branded millions
Who carry through life their faces graven
With sure brute scars that tell the story
Of their foul, fated passions. Science
Has yet no salve to smooth or soften
The cradle-scars of a tyrant's visage;
No drugs to purge from the vital essence
Of souls the sleeping venom. Virtue
May flower in hell, when its roots are twisted
And wound with the roots of vice; but the stronger
Never is known till there comes that battle
With sin to prove the victor. Perilous
Things are these demons we call our passions:
Slaves are we of their roving fancies,
Fools of their devilish glee. — You think me,
I know, in this maundering way designing
To lighten the load of my guilt and cast it
Half on the shoulders of God. But hear me!

I'm partly a man, — for all my weakness, —
If weakness it were to stand and murder
Before men's eyes the man who had murdered
Me, and driven my burning forehead
With horns for the world to laugh at. Trust me!
And try to believe my words but a portion
Of what God's purpose made me! The coward
Within me cries for this; and I beg you
Now, as I come to the end, to remember
That women and men are on earth to travel
All on a different road. Hereafter
The roads may meet. . . . I trust in something —
I know not what. . . .

Well, this was the way of it: —
Stung with the shame and the secret fury
That comes to the man who has thrown his pittance
Of self at a traitor's feet, I wandered
Weeks and weeks in a baffled frenzy,
Till at last the devil spoke. I heard him,
And laughed at the love that strove to touch me, —
The dead, lost love; and I gripped the demon
Close to my breast, and held him, praising
The fates and the furies that gave me the courage
To follow his wild command. Forgetful
Of all to come when the work was over, —
There came to me then no stony vision
Of these three hundred days, — I cherished
An awful joy in my brain. I pondered
And weighed the thing in my mind, and gloried
In life to think that I was to conquer
Death at his own dark door, — and chuckled
To think of it done so cleanly. One evening
I knew that my time had come. I shuddered
A little, but rather for doubt than terror,
And followed him, — led by the nameless devil
I worshipped and called my brother. The city
Shone like a dream that night; the windows
Flashed with a piercing flame, and the pavements
Pulsed and swayed with a warmth — or something

That seemed so then to my feet — and thrilled me
With a quick, dizzy joy; and the women
And men, like marvellous things of magic,
Floated and laughed and sang by my shoulder,
Sent with a wizard motion. Through it
And over and under it all there sounded
A murmur of life, like bees; and I listened
And laughed again to think of the flower
That grew, blood-red, for me! . . . This fellow
Was one of the popular sort who flourish
Unruffled where gods would fall. For a conscience
He carried a snug deceit that made him
The man of the time and the place, whatever
The time or the place might be. Were he sounding,
With a genial craft that cloaked its purpose,
Nigh to itself, the depth of a woman
Fooled with his brainless art, or sending
The midnight home with songs and bottles, —
The cad was there, and his ease forever
Shone with the smooth and slippery polish
That tells the snake. That night he drifted
Into an up-town haunt and ordered —
Whatever it was — with a soft assurance
That made me mad as I stood behind him,
Gripping his death, and waited. Coward,
I think, is the name the world has given
To men like me; but I'll swear I never
Thought of my own disgrace when I shot him —
Yes, in the back, — I know it, I know it
Now; but what if I do? . . . As I watched him
Lying there dead in the scattered sawdust,
Wet with a day's blown froth, I noted
That things were still; that the walnut tables,
Where men but a moment before were sitting,
Were gone; that a screen of something around me
Shut them out of my sight. But the gilded
Signs of a hundred beers and whiskeys
Flashed from the walls above, and the mirrors
And glasses behind the bar were lighted
In some strange way, and into my spirit

A thousand shafts of terrible fire
Burned like death, and I fell. The story
Of what came then, you know.

But tell me,
What does the whole thing mean? What are we, —
Slaves of an awful ignorance? puppets
Pulled by a fiend? or gods, without knowing it?
Do we shut from ourselves our own salvation, —
Or what do we do! I tell you, Dominie,
There are times in the lives of us poor devils
When heaven and hell get mixed. Though conscience
May come like a whisper of Christ to warn us
Away from our sins, it is lost or laughed at, —
And then we fall. And for all who have fallen —
Even for him — I hold no malice,
Nor much compassion: a mightier mercy
Than mine must shrive him. — And I — I am going
Into the light? — or into the darkness?
Why do I sit through these sickening hours,
And hope? Good God! are they hours? — hours?
Yes! I am done with days. And to-morrow —
We two may meet! To-morrow! — To-morrow! . . .

SHOOTING STARS

When ardent summer skies are bright
With myriad friendly lamps that glow
Down from their dark, mysterious height
To charm the shrouded earth below —
Lost in a faith we do not know,
Nor human discord ever jars
With eyes that wide and wider grow,
He sits and waits for shooting stars.

And when they slide across the night
Like arrows from a Titan's bow,
He shudders for supreme delight
And shouts to see them scamper so,

No sneering science comes to show
The poor brain crossed with silly scars;
But flushed with joys that overflow,
He sits and waits for shooting stars.

We call him an unlovely wight;
But if his wit be something slow,
Nor ever weary of the sight
That Adam saw so long ago —
Released from knowledge and its woe,
No gloom his constant rapture mars: —
Oblivious from head to toe,
He sits and waits for shooting stars.

ENVOY

Nor is it yet for us, I trow,
To mock him, or to shut the bars
Of scorn against him — even though
He sits and waits for shooting stars.

OCTAVE

Saints of all times I love, but I love best
The saints that never yet were calendered.
Their silence is my shame, their life my life;
Their pleasure is my pleasure, and their grief
My guide forever. Grief that knows itself
Soon glorifies itself; and some rough man
With no name but his own may tell me more
Of God than all the tomes of printed prayers.

THE IDEALIST

Idealist? — Oh yes, or what you will.
I do not wrangle any more with names —

I only want the Truth. Give me the Truth,
And let the system go; give me the Truth,
And I stand satisfied. Fame, glory, gold, —
Take them, and keep them. They were never mine —
I do not ask for them. I only ask
That I, and you, and you, may get the Truth!

TWO OCTAVES

I

Not by the grief that stuns and overwhelms
All outward recognition of revealed
And righteous omnipresence are the days
Of most of us affrighted and diseased,
But rather by the common snarls of life
That come to test us and to strengthen us
In this the prentice-age of discontent,
Rebelliousness, faint-heartedness, and shame.

II

When through hot fog the fulgid sun looks down
Upon a stagnant earth where listless men
Laboriously dawdle, curse, and sweat,
Disqualified, unsatisfied, inert, —
It seems to me somewhow that God himself
Scans with a close reproach what I have done,
Counts with an unphrased patience my arrears,
And fathoms my unprofitable thoughts.

OCTAVES

I

To get at the eternal strength of things,
And fearlessly to make strong songs of it,

Is, to my mind, the mission of that man
The world would call a poet. He may sing
But roughly, and withal ungraciously;
But if he touch to life the one right chord
Wherein God's music slumbers, and awake
To truth one drowsed ambition, he sings well.

III

To mortal ears the plainest word may ring
Fantastic and unheard-of, and as false
And out of tune as ever to our own
Did ring the prayers of man-made maniacs;
But if that word be the plain word of Truth,
It leaves an echo that begets itself,
Persistent in itself and of itself,
Regenerate, reiterate, replete.

ROMANCE

I

BOYS

We were all boys, and three of us were friends;
And we were more than friends, it seemed to me: —
Yes, we were more than brothers then, we three . . .
Brothers? . . . But we were boys, and there it ends.

II

JAMES WETHERELL

We never half believed the stuff
They told about James Wetherell;
We always liked him well enough,
And always tried to use him well;
But now some things have come to light,
And James has vanished from our view, —
There isn't very much to write,
There isn't very much to do.

LIMERICKS

[1] There was a calm man in Sabattis
Who shot at a skunk through a lattice.
The skunk became dead.
"I got him," he said,
"And now let me see where my hat is."

[2] There's this about the Hindu
He does the best he kin do,
But when he wants
A pair of pants
He has to make his skin do.

[3] There was a pale artist named Ransom,
Whose hands were exceedingly handsome.
To be sure they were seen
He painted them green
And held them all day through the transom.

PLUMMER STREET, GARDINER, MAINE

What are those houses doing in a row?
What is it that makes everything so queer?
Was it a dream of mine, or was it here
Van Amburgh used to come so long ago? —
So long ago? If it was not last year,
When was it, then, the place was all arrayed
With tents and elephants and lemonade,
Lifting-machines, freaks, peanuts, and pop-beer?

Where are they gone now? Tell me, if you can,
Where is the giant? and the tattooed man,
Where are the clowns that once were garrulous?
Where are the people who "performed" on bars?
Where are the targets and "ten-cent cigars"
Gone now? Where is the Hipper Pottamus?

TWILIGHT SONG

[*2 stanzas, following stanza 1*]

We have worked, we have played,
We have won the day's grace,
And at noon through the shade
Read the sun face to face;
We have won the sun's touch,
We have seen the leaf curl,
And we've sold the King's crutch
For a boy and a girl;
We have heard the girl sing
To the tune the Queen made,
We have called the boy King,
We have worked, we have played.

We have loved, we have sung,
We have shared the day's joy,
And the wide skies have rung
With a "long live the Boy!"
We have seen the boy ride
With the King's cloak and spurs,
And the Queen by his side
With the girl's hand in hers;
We've a long way to go,
But the King's knell is rung;
And we're glad now to know
We have loved, we have sung.

NORMANDY

(From the French of Bérat)

When all the land's alive again
With winter far away,
And heaven over France again
Is fairer than to-day,
When springs puts off her gray for green,
And swallows all return —
Then I'll go back to Normandy,
The land where I was born.

I know the fields of Switzerland,
The peaks and icy meres;
I know the skies of Italy,
I know the gondoliers;
But let me wander where I will,
I say that I'll return
To Normandy, my Normandy,
The land where I was born.

At last there comes a time to us
When all dreams lose their glow;
There comes a time when in our souls
We need the long ago;
So when my songs are cold in me,
And love will not return —
Then I'll go back to Normandy,
The land where I was born.

AU REVOIR

(MARCH 23, 1909.)

What libellers of destiny
Are these who are afraid
That something yet without a name
Will seize him in the shade?

Though fever-demons may compound
Their most malefic brew,
No fever can defeat the man
Who still has work to do;

Though mighty lions walk about,
Inimical to see,
No lion yet has ever fed
On things that are to be.

Wherefore, and of necessity,
Will he meet what may come;
And from a nation will be missed
As others are from home.

VARIATIONS OF GREEK THEMES, V

WITH SAPPHO'S COMPLIMENTS

But you are dead now — yes, you are —
And what you say will not go far;
I don't think any one I knew
Was ever quite so dead as you.

I'll say no more, for what remains?
You must have known you had no brains;
For you had nothing but your looks,
And you would never read my books.

So now you'll hate yourself, and hide
Where most ignoble shades abide;
But I'll not make your spirit sad,
For you are dead now — and I'm glad.

BEN JONSON ENTERTAINS A MAN FROM STRATFORD

[*Following line 318*:
"He's fribbling all the time with that damned House."]
But he's not of our time, or any time;
He's of all time. He needs Greek, even at that, —
And a little braver manner with a shilling
O' mornings for the more nefarious
And out o' nights, who are to be forgotten;
Though I'd assure ye — and I'm saying this —
The worthy, for a word, may have his breeches.

NIMMO'S EYES

[*Following stanza 6*]
And think of Nimmo's eyes; and if you can,
Remember something in them that was wrong.
A casual thing to ask of any man,
You tell me, — and you laugh? You won't laugh long.

[*Following stanza 15*]

She makes an epic of an episode,
I tell her, and the toil is ruinous;
And I may tell her till I go the road
We find alone, the best and worst of us.

HANNIBAL BROWN

An Alcaic

Although his wish was never to baffle us
Hannibal Brown was dolichocephalous.
His head reached half way up to heaven.
Hannibal's hat was a number seven.

BROADWAY

By night a gay leviathan
    That fades before the sun —
A monster with a million eyes
    Without the sight of one —
A coruscating thing with claws
    To tear the soul apart —
Breaker of men and avenues,
    It throbs, and has no heart.

By day it has another life
    That feeds on hopes and dreams;
And wears, to cover what it is,
    The mask of what it seems.
But soon its iridescent length
    Will make a fiery show,
To cheer, to dazzle, or to scorch
    The wingless moths below.

And if, at cynic intervals,
    And like a thing in pain,

By chance it implicates itself
    With something not insane,
It will not often, nor for long,
    Relinquish what allures
With everything that has the shine
    Of nothing that endures.

THE PILGRIMS' CHORUS

Long ago there came a sound as of a mighty wind
    from heaven,
And a light was on the world where now it shines
    for us to-day;
We have seen the fire of God as once it fell for men
    before us,
And we follow, knowing only that old things have
    passed away.

Through the weary cloud of years and through the
    dark that was around us
In the west we know the burning of a light across
    the sea;
Through the tumult of a peace that was beyond our
    understanding
We have waited for a voice that we have heard,
    and we are free.

We are free to be the first who are to bear the
    coming harvest
Over leagues that are between us and the fields that
    are unsown;
And though God may leave our reaping unto others
    who come after,
He has called us, and we follow, to the new and
    the unknown.

A WREATH FOR EDWIN MARKHAM

Time, always writing, sees no trace
Of all he writes on Markham's face.
On Markham's face he writes in vain:
Apollo rubs it out again.

TOO MUCH COFFEE

Together in infinite shade
They defy the invincible dawn:
The Measure that never was made,
The Line that never was drawn.

FORTUNATUS

Be as you are; your story is all told,
And all without the cost of augury.
Nothing in years, nothing in chance or fate,
May dent the mail of your complacency.

Be as you are, and always as you are;
Grope for no more than may be requisite.
You are among the chosen of the world
Who serve it best when unaware of it.

For while you see it as it never was,
Your ministration will not be in vain;
You will ameliorate the mystery
Somewhat in seeing so little to explain.

You will not see the drama of dead lives
That are behind calm faces and closed doors;
You will not feel the weight of heavy chains
That others wear that you may not wear yours;

You will not hear the breathing of the beast
That has been history since there was man;
And seeing not much that need be different,
You will not wonder why it all began.

You will not have to see how small a place
Will be enough to make of you a king;
You will have all there is for you to use,
And having little will have everything.

MODRED
A FRAGMENT

Time and the dark
Had come, but not alone. The southern gate
That had been open wide for Lancelot
Made now an entrance for three other men,
Who strode along the gravel or the grass,
Careless of who should hear them. When they came
To the great oak and the two empty chairs,
One paused, and held the others with a tongue
That sang an evil music while it spoke:
"Sit here, my admirable Colgrevance,
And you, my gentle Agravaine, sit here.
For me, well I have had enough of sitting;
And I have heard enough and seen enough
To blast a kingdom into kingdom come,
Had I so fierce a mind — which happily
I have not, for the king here is my father.
There's been a comment and a criticism
Abounding, I believe, in Camelot
For some time at my undeserved expense,
But God forbid that I should make my father
Less happy than he will be when he knows
What I shall have to tell him presently;
And that will only be what he has known
Since Merlin, or the ghost of Merlin, came
Two years ago to warn him. Though he sees,
One thing he will not see; and this must end.

We must have no blind kings in Camelot,
Or we shall have no land worth harrowing,
And our last harvest will be food for strangers.
My father, as you know, has gone a-hunting."

"We know about the king," said Agravaine,
"And you know more than any about the queen.
We are still waiting, Modred. Colgrevance
And I are waiting."

Modred laughed at him
Indulgently: "Did I say more than any?
If so, then inadvertently I erred;
For there is one man here, one Lancelot,
Who knows, I fancy, a deal more than I do,
And I know much. Yes, I know more than much.
Yet who shall snuff the light of what he knows
To blind the king he serves? No, Agravaine,
A wick like that would smoke and smell of treason."

"Your words are mostly smoke, if I may say so,"
Said Colgrevance: "What is it you have seen,
And what are we to do? I wish no ill
To Lancelot. I know no evil of him,
Or of the queen; and I'll hear none of either,
Save what you, on your oath, may tell me now.
I look yet for the trail of your dark fancy
To blur your testament."

"No, Colgrevance,
There are no blurs or fancies exercising
Tonight where I am. Lancelot will ascend
Anon, betimes, and with no drums or shawms
To sound the appointed progress of his feet;
And he will not be lost along the way,
For there are landmarks and he knows them all.
No, Colgrevance, there are no blurs or fancies
Unless it be that your determination
Has made them for your purpose what they seem.
But here I beg your pardon, Colgrevance.

We reticent ones are given to say too much,
With our tongues once in action. Pray forgive.
Your place tonight will be a shadowed alcove,
Where you may see this knight without a stain
While he goes in where no man save the king
Has dared before to follow. Agravaine
And I will meet you on the floor below,
Having already beheld this paragon-Joseph
Go by us for your clinching observation.
Then we, with a dozen or so for strength, will act;
And there shall be no more of Lancelot."

"Modred, I wish no ill to Lancelot,
And I know none of him," said Colgrevance.
"My dream is of a sturdier way than this
For me to serve my king. Give someone else
That alcove, and let me be of the twelve.
I swear it irks the marrow of my soul
To shadow Lancelot — though I may fight him,
If so it is to be. Furthermore, Modred,
You gave me not an inkling of the part
That you have read off now so pleasantly
For me to play. No, Modred, by the God
Who knows the right way and the wrong, I'll be
This night no poisonous inhabitant
Of alcoves in your play, not even for you.
No man were more the vassal of his friend
Than I am, but I'm damned if I'll be owned."

In a becoming darkness Modred smiled
Away the first accession of his anger.
"Say not like that," he answered, musically.
"Be temperate, Colgrevance. Remember always
Your knighthood and your birth. Remember, too,
That I may hold him only as my friend
Who loves me for myself, not for my station.
We're born for what we're born for, Colgrevance;
And you and I and Agravaine are born
To serve our king. It's all for the same end,
Whether we serve in alcoves, or behind

A velvet arras on another floor.
What matters it, if we be loyal men —
With only one defection?"

"Which is — what?"
Said Agravaine, who breathed hard and said little,
Albeit he had no fame abroad for silence.

"Delay — procrastination — overcaution —
Or what word now assimilates itself
The best with your inquiring mood, my brother.
These operations that engage us now
Were planned and executed long ago,
Had I but acted then on what was written
No less indelibly than at this hour,
Though maybe not so scorchingly on me.
'If there were only Modred in the way,' —
I heard her saying it — 'would you come tonight?'
Saint Brandan! How she nuzzled and smothered him!
Forgive me, Colgrevance, when I say more
Than my raw vanity may reconcile
With afterthought. But that was what she said
To Lancelot, and that was what I heard.
And what I saw was of an even bias
With all she told him here. God, what a woman!
She floats about the court so like a lily,
That even I'd be fooled were I the king,
Seeing with his eyes what I would not see.
But now the stars are crying in their courses
For this to end, and we are men to end it.
Meanwhile, for the king's hunting and his health,
We have tonight a sort of wassailing;
Wherefore we may as well address ourselves,
Against our imminent activities,
To something in the way of trencher service —
Which also is a service to the king.
For they who serve must eat. God save the King!"

They took the way of Lancelot along
The darkened hedges to the palace lights,

With Modred humming lowly to himself
A chant of satisfaction. Colgrevance,
Not healed of an essential injury,
Nor given the will to cancel his new pledge
To Modred, made with neither knowing why,
Passed in without a word, leaving his two
Companions hesitating on the steps
Outside, one scowling and the other smiling.

"Modred, you may have gone an inch too far
With Colgrevance tonight. Why set a trap
For trouble? We've enough with no additions.
His fame is that of one among the faithful,
Without a fear, and fearless without guile."

"And that is why we need him, Agravaine,"
Said Modred, with another singing laugh.
"He'll go as was appointed by his fate
For my necessity. A man to achieve
High deeds must have a Colgrevance or two
Around him for unused emergencies,
And for the daily sweat. Your Colgrevance
May curse himself till he be violet,
Yet he will do your work. There is none else,
Apparently, that God will let him do."

"Not always all of it," said Agravaine.
But Modred answered with another laugh
And led the way in to the wassailing,
Where Dagonet was trolling a new song
To Lancelot, who smiled — as if in pain
To see so many friends and enemies,
All cheering him, all drinking, and all gay.

PROSE

BORES

Looking back into the dark ages, when the stake and block nearly ruled the world, when a man was put to the rack for some trivial offense, which at the present day would hardly attract notice, and multitudes were burned at the stake for some religious difference, and then turning to the present, we marvel at the change.

The advancing centuries brought with them a civilization which pictured before the people the deeds of former days; the tortures were gradually abandoned, and people slowly gained their rights. Their deeds no longer appeared as just punishment of crime, but as a dark blot on progress, justice and civilization.

Man's duty on this earth is the performance of that which will benefit not only himself, but the community. He should work for his own interest, but at the same time for the public good; he should learn and act accordingly; he should obey the laws and live peaceably; he should mind his own business.

This is what he should do: Travel over the country, or read the daily papers and histories, and see what he does; visit the slums and narrow alleys of our great cities, and draw his own conclusions at the signs of degradation on every hand.

"There among the glooming alleys, progress halts with palsied foot."

No nation can progress as rapidly when continually harassed by events which butt against the walls of justice; no individual can succeed as well when constantly held back by some outside matter. If we can imagine the state of the nation fifty years hence, enlightened by fifty years of experiment and study, could we imagine it free from obstacles, which in themselves amount to nothing, but by their numbers assume the form of a snag, blocking the paths of civilization?

In every city, town and village (this city not excepted), there is always to be found a brigade whose food consists of other people's affairs, who are always ready to predict marriages for months ahead, who can always find some fault with another's new bonnet, who delight in sending out a corps of urchins after votes, providing the place is large enough to hold a fair.

Even in country villages people sometimes die, and then there is a funeral. Does it not seem a sufficient trial to bear the loss of a friend, without being compelled to listen to a three or four hours' harangue by a preacher who reviews everything, from the fall of Adam to the Cambridge strike, and supposes he is teaching some great moral lesson, but at the end is no nearer his point than when he began? It is truly said, "many a minister is the undertaker of the subject he undertakes."

At the present day the world is overflowing with a light class of literature, much of which in material has the same ideas and ends, usually spun to a tiresome length, and containing page after page of description, which is copied almost verbatim into each book the author writes. The excessive perusal of this line of literature blunts the mind of the reader, who in a short time can appreciate no other style. The excessive sale encourages the production, and any one can see the result.

So it may be found in every phase of life. One man takes things as they come, and makes the best of it; another is continually growling, and throws a dark shadow between himself and every one he meets.

Now the entire category of these disciples of Reversion should be bound together by a withe twisted from their own actions, tagged for Astolat, (the crippled servitor once more called out,) and sent "upward with the flood."

A BOOK OF VERSE THAT IS POETRY

Every critical reader of poetry, or of anything else, must involuntarily establish for himself a more or less definite standard whereby to discriminate between mediocrity and the real thing; and when this reader finds a modern poem that has in it more of the real thing than mediocrity, he feels that he has discovered something worth while. And he who discovers or in [any] way gets possession of *The Wayfarers,* by

Miss Josephine Preston Peabody, cannot but feel that the real thing has been accomplished.

This does not necessarily imply that Miss Peabody has written a great book, or even a great poem; but it does imply that she has done something quite out of the ordinary. This may not, from the severer point of view, be startlingly high praise; but from the point of view of contemporary verse-making, it is practically equivalent to saying there is no writer in America to-day who is qualified to inspire Miss Peabody with any great amount of poetical awe. Her book may not commend itself to that exclusive majority which reads poetry "only for the thought;" but it is not, on the other hand, in any way to be identified with the rather distressing product of the school whose watchword is a self-confessed fallacy known as "art for art's sake" — whatever that may be. Art is a means to an end, and Miss Peabody is fortunate enough to know it. Consequently her work is neither form without substance, nor substance without form, but an artistic combination of the two — a combination which must occur wherever there is to be real literature.

These two things, however, are not in themselves enough to make poetry. There must be imagination and sympathy, there must be spirituality and wisdom. Miss Peabody's imagination is not of the pounding, pyrotechnic sort that has made so many ephemeral reputations for its victims; nor is her spirituality of that irrational, unsubstantial kind that causes so many lovely first editions to disappear from the mental gaze of mortals like colorless toy-balloons, — but she has imagination, and she has spirituality, and she has the other things.

The first and longest poem, from which the book takes its attractive title, contains much to praise and very little to condemn — nothing in fact beyond a few feminine vagaries of rhetoric which the author will outgrow. The following stanzas, which are no better than many others that might be chosen, will speak for themselves:—

XVIII

She sat where all the high-roads meet
  And all the striving ways are one.

The dumb sea crept unto her feet
With lowered mane, his wrath undone.
The voice of all the worlds astir
Sunk to the past at sight of her.
There was naught left but her blind eyes that gazed into the climbing sun.

XX

She spake: "I am that One ye sought
Through years that fade, through ways that wind.
I am that One for whom ye wrought
The lovely names ye thought to find:
'Life, the Revealer, whom we reach
Her mother knees, shall smile to teach
Her soul to us.' And would I not, if I but knew! But I am blind.

XXI

"Yet by the stranger gifts ye bring,
And by your alien prayers that throng,
I know I am not that ye sing,
The little dream that does me wrong.
Ye pray me that I shew you what
My one name is: I know it not;
Only I know I am not Death, I am not Love, I am not Song.

XXIII

"They dream I sit on high, afar,
A light to pierce all mystery;
Untroubled as a fixèd star
That heeds no sorrow of the sea.
Yet stars make patient pilgrimage
Across the dark, from age to age;
And who would know me that I am, must take my hand and go with me."

There are thirty of these stanzas in the whole poem, and all of them are good. The closing one is particularly good, with just enough of reminiscent flourish in it to give the desired culminating effect without an overshow of consciousness:—

XXX

I know not if the years be years,
As, great and small, we journey on,
Nor if the service of the spheres
And of the friendly weeds be one . . .
Like singing harvesters, that fare
Weary and glad, we go where'er
She leads the way, with strong, blind eyes, that dare to gaze into the sun.

As there is much to praise in this opening poem, so is there much to praise in the seventy pages that follow it — though there may be a little more to condemn in the way of occasional extravagance and repetition. It is devoutly to be wished that the writer will in her next volume abjure such words as "glamourie" and "enringing" for instance. "Glamourie" may be a matter of taste, but "enringing," when used twice as a rhyming word in a small volume, is a rhetorical crime. "Fade along the hush of air, Burden of the weed," may be all right, but certain disreputable and irreverent readers who are given to smoke pipes in silent places will almost inevitably misinterpret it. These, like many others that might be pointed out, are little faults, but they are the very faults which are likely to be magnified by the casual reader. Books of verse are not exactly novelties nowadays, and it behooves the writer of one to be wary in the printing of anything that may possibly give a totally wrong impression of the book as a whole.

But there is nothing to be misinterpreted or questioned in a poem like the following, in which there is a union of art and substance, of wisdom and imagination, that amounts almost, if not quite, to genius:—

JONGLEUR

Ah, ye that loved my laughter once,
  Open to me! 'Tis I
That shed you songs like summer leaves
  Whenever a wind came by.
The leaves are spent and the year is old,
And the fields are gray that once were gold.
Heart of the brook, my heart is cold—
  My song is like to die.

The windows look another way,
  The walls are deaf and stark.
Who heeds a glow-worm in the day,
  Or lifts a frozen lark?
Warm yourself with the days that were;
Follow the Summer, beg of her,
But never sadden us, Jongleur,
Jongleur, go down the dark!

Poems like *The Fishers, The Weavers, Canonized, Daphne Laurea,* and the *Envoy* might be quoted as more powerful, more significant, but this little song is enough to illustrate the author's method of uniting something to say with an artist's ability to say it. The *Envoy* is unnecessarily modest, but "the wisdom of the one day more" will require a good deal of patience and hard work for its adequate poetical expression. If Miss Peabody is willing to do this work, and refuses to be flattered into doing too much of the kind of thing that usually follows the publication of a successful first book, her next appearance will be a literary event—without quotation marks.

THE BALM OF CUSTOM

There are thousands of excellent Democrats who will vote for Mr. Bryan this fall because they have "got used to him." They will not vote for him because they have made a logical analysis — so far as such a thing is possible — of his curiously complicated ethics; they will not vote for him because they believe that Bryanism, as a rejuvenating abstraction, is the one thing that will save this Western world from damnation and eclipse. But they will vote for him, and they will do it because he is no longer an object of unqualified terror to them. They will take him as a matter of course. They will take him somewhat as an uncomplaining farmer would take a blight or a long drouth — as a part of the Great Plan.

It is much easier to vote than it is to think, and it is far more restful to yield to the subtile magnetism of a good old word like Democrat than it is to dedicate a few "sessions of sweet, silent thought" to finding out what the word means as it is used to-day in the United States of America. No honest man would encourage any illusions in regard to the simplicity of such an undertaking, but one might venture to wish that some of his pacific fellow countrymen would at least put to themselves the question of the immortal Congressman who did not know where he was "at." They are not silver men, they are "not exactly anti-imperialists"; they are just Democrats. They do not show specific symptoms of even the most remote forms of Bryanistic unrest; they do not seem to be more than casually restless over anything. Marjorie Fleming would say that they are more than usually calm. They did not vote for Bryan in 1896, for he was a novelty then and they were afraid of him; but they will vote for him in 1900, for he is no longer a novelty and they are no longer afraid of him. Custom has so staled his infinite monotony that he does not seem to them to be half so dangerous as he used to be.

They are willing enough to confess that Mr. Bryan has a few peculiar attributes that are not wholly admirable, and some of them will say that they have occasional suggestions of something like doubt as to the alleged infallibility of his prophetic genius. They have heard that he can read the future as well as an ordinary man can read a newspaper, and a few of them may have heard that his persistent association with "things that are to be" has been bad for his sense of proportion, and positively shocking to his realization of the prophetic significance of things that are. But all this need not dishearten them. It is said that Michelangelo, after completing his work on the ceiling of the Sistine Chapel, could not read a book with any comfort without holding it above his head; and if this be true of Michelangelo, what may not be true of Mr. Bryan? If so slight a task as that of painting Biblical allegories on a ceiling may produce such strange results, what may not be the results of trying to decorate the zenith with all sorts of pictorial fables that will not stick? And who is to wonder that Mr. Bryan should be impatient and somewhat irrational? Not these reclaimed and passive supporters of his, assuredly. It is not their duty to wonder; it is their duty to be consistent Democrats. It is just as easy to be consistent as it is to be incredulous.

And therefore they will vote. They will not know precisely what they are voting for, but they will not be annoyed by a little discrepancy like that. They have relaxed themselves into a state of intellectual captivity that has developed [by] degrees into a condition that borders on political Nirvana, and Nirvana is nothing if not painless. Four solid years have been given to them for the attainment of this individual negation, and they appear to have improved every hour of it; they have got used to Mr. Bryan and they are going to do their duty; and they seem to be contented. There is a great deal in getting used to things. The illustrious Lord Byron wrote a famous poem about a man who got so used to being a captive that he regained his freedom with a sigh.

AUTOBIOGRAPHICAL SKETCHES: HARVARD

Born	*Head Tide, Me., Dec. 22, 1869.*
Parents	*Edward Robinson, Mary Elizabeth Palmer.*
School	*High School, Gardiner, Me.*
Years in College	*1891-1893.*
Occupation	*Author.*
Address	*99 John St., care of Ledoux and Company, New York, N. Y.*

I do not find that I have much to say for myself, or of myself, except that I have done literary work since leaving Harvard in 1893. I have written from time to time for the magazines, and I have published the following books of verse: *The Torrent and the Night Before,* (privately printed in 1896), *The Children of the Night,* (Badger, 1897; Scribner, 1905), *Captain Craig,* (Houghton, Mifflin Co., 1902); Macmillan, 1915), *The Town Down the River* (Scribner, 1905). I have also published a play in three acts called *Van Zorn,* (Macmillan, 1914). I wrote this play — calling it by mistake a comedy — primarily to please myself; and I seem therein to have succeeded admirably. Several well-known "theatrical people" have praised it highly; but none of them has said anything about putting it on the stage. If this begins to read to you (meaning the secretary and the editor) like an advertisement, I can only say that you should not have asked me for more than I wrote you in reply to your first request for information. I might add that certain superficial critics who have called me a pessimist have been entirely wrong in their diagnosis. In point of fact, one has only to read my books to wish that half the world might have half my optimism. Member: Institute of Arts and Letters. [1915]

I find that I have not much to say for myself, or of myself, except that I have done literary work since leaving Harvard in 1893. I have written from time to time for the magazines, and I have published several books of verse. I might add that certain superficial critics who have called me a pessimist have been entirely wrong in their diagnosis. In point of fact,

I recommend a careful reading of my books to any one who wishes to become an incurable optimist. My 'principal hatreds,' or two of them, are prohibition and free verse. [1920]

"Still writing," Edwin Arlington Robinson notes on his blanks. That is his modest way of putting it. The list of his publications includes almost one volume of poetry a year. In 1922 his *Collected Poems* won the Pulitzer Prize of $1000 for the best book of verse by an American author during that year. He was awarded the Pulitzer Prize again in 1924 for *The Man Who Died Twice,* another volume of verse. You never would have guessed this from his letter, however. He merely says:

"I have nothing very exciting to report, my life having gone on without many changes. I am beginning to realize that fifty-five is not so very different from twenty-five, except that one can't eat and drink everything in sight as he once could. They made a Litt.D. of me at Yale four years ago, and I have loafed three months in London twice since. That's about all." [1925]

MUSIC AND POETRY

I find it rather difficult to say anything tangible or satisfactory about the relation of music and poetry — music being poetry, and poetry being music. Not long ago I attempted, in a newspaper interview, to define poetry as "a language that tells us, through a more or less emotional reaction, something that cannot be said." This might be an equally good, or bad, definition of music, but for the fact that the reader would balk instinctively at the qualifying "more or less" before "emotional" — the emotional reaction in the case of music that endures being unquestionably "more." And this, no doubt, is equally true of much of the best poetry, although it seems to me that words, in their very nature, no matter how intense or lyrical their expression, must obviously admit of subtleties of sound and sense that would not be possible in any conceivable combination of tones. As a layman, I cannot resist this opportunity to make myself offensive by setting down my by no means original belief that most of the present-day composers are carefully insuring oblivion for their names and their notes by forcing tones to do the work of words. On the other hand, it is equally true that many poets — Swinburne and Lanier, for example — have gone altogether too far in trying to make words do the work of tones. Generally speaking, I should be inclined to say that the field of poetry is infinitely more various and less definable than that of music, for the simple reason that poetry is language and music at the same time. There is no such thing as "programme" poetry, and some of us are almost willing to wish there might be no more "programme" music. Poetry has been called for centuries the greatest of the arts, but I should rather say that music and poetry are two — or rather three — manifestations of the greatest of the arts. At any rate this arrangement would leave the musician happy with a right to say that music (meaning tone) begins where poetry (meaning language) leaves off. But the tones of music will have to go faster and farther than they have yet gone if they expect or hope to keep the overtones of language far behind them.

THE PETERBOROUGH IDEA

In one of Bret Harte's romantic parodies—in that of Dumas *père,* I believe—the exaggerated hero works himself into a state of desperation over the lack of a ladder just thirty-seven feet long, and suddenly trips over something in the grass that proves to be a ladder just thirty-seven feet long. If the number of feet was not thirty-seven, it was some other number; and it was one that was in exact accord with the exaggerated hero's romantic necessities. And if this introduction seems irrelevant, let me say that in the Spring of 1911 I found myself in a situation not extravagantly unlike that of the aforesaid hero, save that my problem was far more complicated, and if anything less favorably designed for immediate solution; for I found myself in possession of a thing I was pleased to call an Idea for a Work of Art, and one that required, for its most advantageous working out, a combination of conditions that was not promised by the sights, smells, temperatures, and noises of New York City during the Summer months, or by any enforced seclusion that I had then in mind.

What I required, or at least wished for, was a place in the country, not too far from the civilizing conveniences of life, that would afford comfortable lodging, good food, a large and well-windowed sleeping room with a good bed in it, an easy walk to breakfast at about seven-thirty, a longer walk to a secluded and substantial building in the woods, a large open fireplace and plenty of fuel, a free view from the door of the best kind of New England scenery, a complete assurance of a long day before me without social annoyances or interruptions of any kind, a simple luncheon brought to my door by a punctual but reticent carrier, a good dinner at night with a few congenial people, an evening without enforced solitude or enforced society, and a blessed assurance that no one would ask me to show him or her what I was writing.

Having attracted the attention of Destiny to these few casual suggestions, it occurred to me that Destiny might have to move perceptibly out of its way in order to fulfill them all at once; and I had trained myself to forget pretty much all about them, when it happened that I met a literary friend of mine to whom I repeated a few of them. I might have repeated all of them, but all of them were not necessary. The two suggestions of complete solitude during the day and of a house in the woods were sufficient to bring about my realization not only of those two, but of all the others—not to mention several more that I have not had the assurance or the complacency to set down. "Why don't you try the MacDowell Colony?" he asked. "Colony?" I repeated after him. "Does a friend of mine talk to me of 'colonies' when I tell him that what I want is a commodious house in the woods, preferably with a cement floor, and with no one to bother me between eight or nine in the morning and six at night? What are friends good for anyhow?" "Do you know anything about the place?" he ventured, I thought a little timidly. "No," I said, "except that it is a 'colony': and that's enough." "Do you believe," he rejoined, "that Edward MacDowell would have encouraged the kind of 'colony' that you seem to have in mind?" I had to admit that such a belief was a difficult one to entertain; and I succumbed to the extent of listening to him while he painted again the picture that was in my dreams. I did not believe much of what he said, but I listened to him because he was a friend of mine and because he had written some things that I liked.

Well, the result of my friend's insistence was a reluctant journey on my part from New York to Peterborough, New Hampshire, with a long and pusillanimous halt in Boston— where I could be sure of my ground, even if I could not have there a stone house in the woods, with seven screened windows and a screen door that opened on the peak of Mount Monadnock seven miles away. Finally, when I realized that the Fourth of July had come and gone, and that summer was going after it, I found out how to get to Peterborough and in three hours I was there; but only after a dubious and rather unhappy ride, during which I was pursued and haunted unceasingly by the ominous word "colony," which buzzed and bit me like an obnoxious insect that might have hatched itself from the worm that smote the gourd of Jonah. Colonies of ants or colonies of microbes I could tolerate, but colonies of artists and writers were too much for the contemplation of a "difficult" poet who had a small but intensely select public that was said to be growing. I believed that I might possibly stay in Peterborough for as long as two weeks, at the end of which time I should call upon my alleged creative faculty for some elaborate lie that would insure my quiet if ignominious escape. But my escape did not go into effect until the end of the following September, when I was called back to New York, after having worked for nearly three months in uninterrupted harmony with all the suggestions that I had filed with Destiny, not much expecting to hear from them again. I found here not only what my friend said that I should find, but infinitely and surprisingly more.

I found nearly everything that I did not much expect to find, and hardly anything that my conventional doubts had anticipated. For about a week I employed myself in trying not to enjoy my liberty and solitude, and in being glad that I was not in New York. But one may do these things almost anywhere in the country. I knew that, and I knew there must be something unusual about the place, or I should not like it when I was trying so hard not to like it. I knew there was something that I had not yet found, and I learned what it was when one day I discovered, rather of a sudden, that the MacDowell Colony was beyond a doubt the worst loafing place in the world. I had loafed now for more than a week, but I had not rested. I did not begin to rest until I began to work; and it was not until I began to work that I began to understand what had been the matter with me. Hitherto my long-suffering conscience—a New England conscience at that—had never made any special fuss to remind me of so banal a thing as lost opportunity. I had lost so much and so many kinds of opportunity that I supposed my conscience had become calloused on the industrial side, and had ceased to respond to this particular defection on my part. But I was woefully wrong. During the next ten weeks I did more work, got more out of living and out of nature, and became better acquainted with myself than during any part of the past three or four years. And fortunately for me, by nature and long training one of the laziest of mortals, I was early in realizing that this long desired opportunity of mine to get away for awhile from the world and to express a part of what the world had given me, was the direct and almost immediate result of what was once a thought in the mind of a man who had foreseen what all this might mean some day to others. In his own life it was hardly more than a persistent wish. Today it is five hundred acres of land and a score of substantial buildings, nearly all of which are invisible to the tenants of the others.

Before I try to say what the Peterborough Idea is, I should like to say as gently as possible a few things that it most emphatically is *not*. In view of some of the more grotesque and pathetic misconceptions concerning it, it may be well to say at once that it is not a school, or a sanitarium, or a summer resort for incurable amateurs, or an experiment in misapplied aesthetics, or a kind of protracted and intensified afternoon tea. As a matter of fact afternoon tea is not encouraged, although it has not yet been entirely eradicated. There are no "students," for the simple reason that there is no place for them. There are no teachers, or professors, or advisers. There are no bells, and there are no "hours." There are no amateurs, until they are found out; and they are found out in Peterborough as in other places. Perhaps they are found out in Peterborough a little sooner than in other places. There are no annoying regulations to irritate the most sensitive and responsive talent, or to interfere with the most robust and uncompromising genius. I have said that the MacDowell Colony is in all probability the worst loafing place in the world. It is also, in all probability, about the worst place in which to conceal one's lack of a creative faculty. With each year the place becomes automatically more exclusive (I use the word, of course, in its serious and literal sense), and with each year come fewer—there were never many—of those who would, and eventually do, find a more congenial and inspiring environment elsewhere. And it is not intended that more than twenty or twenty-five people shall ever be working here at the same time.

But misconceptions are a part of the burden that must always be borne by those who undertake something that is radically different from anything that the public has known before, and the philosophical and tolerant creator of the Peterborough Colony accepts them with angelic forbearance and good humor. If there is one of these many misconceptions that annoys her more than another, probably it is the prevailing delusion that the place is intended primarily, if not exclusively, for the impecunious—the truth being that the question of money has nothing whatever to do with the advantages that are offered. Some of the best work that has been done here has been done by artists and writers of recognized standing, with incomes sufficient to render the financial side of their advantages a negligible matter. On the other hand some of the best work has been done by those whose incomes are still more or less problematical — a fact that has hardly sufficient novelty to inaugurate a new epoch in the history of the Fine Arts. The basic purpose of the place is not to foster the "promise" of a few indigent neophytes, or to soothe the shattered hopes of a few indigent wrecks. On the contrary, neophytes and wrecks are alike ineligible.

The MacDowell Colony is, let me say again, the splendid

outgrowth of a thought that was long in the mind of the most serious, the most scholarly, the most inspired, and probably the most thoroughly sophisticated of American composers. It is not easy to associate the name and the ideals of Edward MacDowell with the encouragement of mediocrity, or with the frittering away of time and opportunity that offer almost incredible advantages alike to the poor and to the independent. Money cannot buy elsewhere what is offered by the MacDowell Colony in Peterborough to the serious worker, and the reason for this is that what is offered in Peterborough to the serious worker does not exist elsewhere. If it does exist elsewhere, I have never found it; and I have worked, I fancy, under what might be called a fairly representative variety of favorable and unfavorable conditions.

It is practically impossible for me to say, even to myself, just what there is about this place that compels a man to work out the best that is in him, and to be discontented if he fails to do so. The abrupt and somewhat humiliating sense of isolation, liberty, and opportunity which overtakes one each morning has something to do with it, but this sense of opportunity does not in itself explain everything. There is, over and about the place, a mystical touch that cannot be explained any more than MacDowell's *Keltic Sonata* can be explained. The presence of a great genius is always here, although the man himself is absent; and this presence is not one to confirm or foster any unhappy misconceptions in regard to charity-patients or incorrigible amateurs. The place is a workshop, not a wonderland; or perhaps I might better call it a workshop with a wonderland thrown in. But one must work and be in earnest, and he must know that others know that he is in earnest, or the wonderland will give him but a sorry sort of pleasure. The few who have attempted to forego the workshop for the wonderland have not had a very good time, and they are not likely to come again.

The place is not only a workshop, but one for those who have already achieved something that contemporary criticism believes to be important. Contemporary criticism makes a great many sad mistakes, no doubt, but contemporary achievement can have no other judge or sponsor; and for this reason some of those who have achieved what is in them to achieve will always be advanced in their own time beyond their deserts, while others may be long submerged, and finally exterminated, for lack of opportunity.

Now the purpose of this place is to furnish that opportunity to those whom the best of contemporary criticism has accepted as a matter of course, and to those who are said by experts to deserve it: that is the Peterborough Idea. Nature has a great deal to say in these matters, and probably there is no place where she says more to the man or woman who has already done something significant than she says here in Peterborough. The mere fact that a man or a woman has written a few books, or painted a few pictures, or composed a few songs, or modeled a few images in clay, means little or nothing nowadays among intelligent people. In fact, it is coming to be rather a distinction not to have done one or more of these things—unless one has done something sufficiently forceful and original to be suggestive, at least, of endurance. For the world must have its art, or the world will be no fit place for man to live in; and the artist must have his opportunity, or his art will die and the artist will die with it.

A great deal of well-meaning nonsense has been said and written about the so-called selfishness of the creative faculty, but a small reading of history should be enough to indicate some fraction of the price that has been paid by the creator, in most instances, for his indulgence of that selfishness. In the opinion of many, a good artist is like a good Indian; and he will probably remain so. At any rate, it was with this probability in mind that the creator of the Peterborough Colony as it is today, Mrs. Edward MacDowell, found herself ready and eager to sacrifice everything else for the unselfish and effective realization of what was once a thought in the mind of Edward MacDowell, and is now five hundred acres of land, partly farm but largely forest, and a score of detached and carefully constructed buildings that have a gratifying suggestion of permanence.

I fancy that Mrs. MacDowell is tired of praise, and that she is wishing to herself that the confidence and the encouragement of some of her admirers might begin to assume another form. But there is no need of my dwelling upon the obvious. If I have given my readers a nearer picture of the place than they had before, and a clearer notion of what it means and is going to mean, I shall at least have corrected for them a few of the more fantastic and unfortunate errors that have long been circulated in regard to an enterprise that has been from its inception in accord with everything that is rational, natural and desirable.

THE NEW MOVEMENT IN POETRY

You ask me if I think there is a new movement in poetry, and my reply is that there is always a new movement in poetry. There is always a new movement in everything, including each new inch of each new revolution of the earth around the sun. But if you mean to ask me if this new movement implies necessarily any radical change in the structure or in the general nature of what the world has agreed thus far to call poetry, I shall have to tell you that I do not think so — knowing very well that my answer is worth no more than that of any other relatively intelligent individual.

In referring to a new movement I assume that you refer primarily to *vers libre* — a form, or lack of form, that may or may not produce pleasant results. I do not know that there is any final reason why this mode of expression should not give pleasure as often as any other, although I do know, so far as I am concerned, that in the majority of cases it does not. I have read furlongs of it, but the amount that has given me any solid satisfaction could easily be measured in a few yards at the most. I say this with reluctance, for I know that some of my friends will disagree with me entirely, and be tempted in all probability to call me names. Some of them may call me a conservative, others a reactionary; and all this in spite of the fact that I have been accused in the past of being, if anything, too modern. But these accusations were made long ago; and I fancy that my limited public has come by this time to see that I was never so perilously modern, after all.

If there be a new movement in poetry that can be definitely labeled, such a movement will probably be found to have more to do with vocabulary and verbal arrangement than with metrical or non-metrical form. The poetry of the next few hundred years will in all probability have an incisiveness and a clarity that have not generally prevailed heretofore, and some of the best of it may be written in *vers libre*; although my own opinion is that most of the best of it will be written in some form or other that shall have a definite metrical pattern. I may be grievously in the wrong, yet it seems to me that up to this time *vers libre* has been its own worst indictment, in that perhaps less than one per cent of it may be said to possess the quality that gives pleasure. In spite of the fact that it has produced several interesting and stimulating results, I am inclined to the belief that the *vers libre* movement has seen its best days, and that the few writers who have succeeded in making it interesting are still to do their best work along more traditional lines, in which there is room for any amount of innovation and variety. But, as I said before, my opinion is merely that of an individual, possibly prejudiced, and is, therefore, to be taken as such and as nothing more.

In reply to your request for a criticism of contemporary American literature, perhaps I had better keep to the subject of poetry and express my belief in the genuineness of its "revival" and in the significance of much that has been published during the past few years.

MY METHODS AND MEANINGS

I am handicapped at the start in having no biography and no theories. You will find as much in *Who's Who* as I have to say about myself personally; and as for my work, I have hoped that it might speak — not very loudly, perhaps — for itself. Ten years ago I was called a radical, and most readers looked sideways at my work on account of its unconventional use of so-called simple language. I suppose that I have always depended rather more on context than on vocabulary for my poetical effects, and this offense has laid me open to the charge of over-subtlety on the part of the initiated and of dullness on the part of the dull. Whatever merit my work may or may not possess, I fancy that it will always be a waste of time for any reader who has not a fairly well developed sense of humor — which, as someone has said before, is a very serious thing — to bother with it. When I tell you that my poem called "The Gift of God" (in *The Man Against the Sky*) has been interpreted as a touching tribute to our Saviour, you will require no further comment upon this point.

When I was younger, I was very much under the influence of Wordsworth and Kipling, but never at all, so far as I am aware, under that of Browning, as many seem to believe. As a matter of fact, I have never been able to understand the alleged resemblance unless it can be attributed to my use of rather more colloquial language than "poetic diction" has usually sanctioned. I began the writing of verse long before I was old enough to know better, and I fancy that I am safe in saying that my style, such as it is, was pretty well formed by the time my first book was published, in 1896.

As for my methods of work, there does not seem to be much for me to say. As a rule I see the end of a thing before I begin it (if I don't see it then, I am likely never to see it) and the rest of the process is simply a matter of how the thing goes. Sometimes it goes rapidly, sometimes slowly; and so far as I can see, one method produces about the same result as the other, provided I know what I am trying to say. When occasionally I have become disgusted and thrown an unfinished poem away, it has always been because I had really nothing to write about. I have written a sonnet in twenty minutes as a joke ("Another Dark Lady") and I have tinkered others ("The Clerks," for example) for a month. Generally speaking, I should be inclined to say that if some sort of first draft doesn't form itself rather quickly, the final product is likely to be unsatisfactory; but with something definite and worth while to work on, any amount of labor may justify itself. Again, it may not. I imagine, however, that the worst poetry in the world has been written in the finest frenzy of inspiration; and so, probably, has the best.

When you ask me to annotate individual poems, I find myself in another difficulty. While nearly everything that I have written has a certain amount of personal coloring, I do not recall anything of mine that is a direct transcription of experience. For example, I have never liked the sound of church-bells; and the sound of their ringing one evening for the wedding of two people in whom I had not the remotest interest brought about a mood in me that made me write "On the Night of a Friend's Wedding" — a sonnet, by the way, that was begun suddenly, and later worked over for an immoderate length of time. But I was younger then than I am now, and time didn't count.

I thought nothing when I was writing my first book of working for a week over a single line; and while I don't do it any more, I am sure that my technique is better for those early grilling exercises. In fact, I am now more than inclined to believe that the technical flabbiness of many writers is due to the lack in earlier years of just such grilling — in the years when one is not conscious of how hard he is working and of how much time he is wasting — unless he is ready to gamble his life away for the sake of winning the possible conjunction of a few inevitable words. It seems an odd stake to play for so heavily, and perhaps it is fortunate for the race that so few are playing for it. Of course almost everyone is writing verse nowadays, but not many are taking it seriously enough to let it interfere with their meal tickets.

I haven't my books at hand, but for poems to read aloud you might consider "John Evereldown," "The Tavern," "The Clerks," "Amaryllis" (*Children of the Night*) ; "Morgan and Fingal," "Cortège" (*Captain Craig*) ; "The Master," the "Calvary" poem, "Vickery's Mountain" from *The Town Down the River;* "Doctor of Billiards" (which, by the way, is not a plea for the suppression of vice) ; and whatever you like from *The Man Against the Sky* — "Flammonde" and "The Gift of God," perhaps. The end of "Master" might possibly give pleasure. . . .

The poems that I have cited do not seem to require any explanation — with the exception perhaps of "Vickery's Mountain," which is after all merely a study of human inertia, which is in Vickery's case something stronger than he is. Flammonde is the man who sees but cannot do for himself, "others he saved," etc. "John Evereldown" and "The Tavern" are purely fanciful sketches, without ethical or symbolical significance. "Doctor of Billiards" pictures a man who seems to be throwing away a life which, for some reason known only to himself, is no longer worth living. "The Man Against the Sky" is a protest against a material explanation of the universe. "Morgan and Fingal" is merely an episode with overtones.

A NEW ENGLAND POET

I am sure that the name of Alanson Tucker Schumann, whose recent death in Florida has been reported, will be missed by many readers of the *Transcript* who have read for the past twenty-five years the singularly polished and accomplished verses of this competent, though unostentatious, New England poet. By profession a physician in Gardiner, Me., he still found time to live what was probably to him the best part of his life in the land of fancy—a land where he saw much that others might not have seen. Dr. Schumann, with his highly responsive sense of beauty and his quiet sense of humor, seems to have had a rare and happy way of finding poetry in almost everything; and his expression of it was more than often something near to perfect. It is difficult, for example, to foresee oblivion for a sonnet like the following, which is altogether remarkable for its cumulative poetic volume:

GUIDANCE

Upon the corner of a village street,
Close to the limits of my homestead lands,
An unpretentious upright firmly stands,
In workmanship plain, commonplace and neat.
To make its purpose clear, its form complete,
Below its top, like fingerless still hands,
A lettered board, transversely placed, commands
To the right path the stranger's doubting feet.

And when the vision widens, and the stars
Majestically move across the night,
And God seems near in their eternal glow—
When no harsh voice the sacred silence mars,
I see, beyond the structure's slender height,
The shadow of a Cross upon the snow.

And this intimate if less ambitious example of the clarity of his method may be found, choosing almost at random from his one published book, *The Man and the Rose,* in a sonnet like

"Deane's Grove," which is obviously autobiographical and sincere:

DEANE'S GROVE

I went for acorns one October day
Into a grove—Deane's Grove we called it then.
It was my time of happy childhood when
All sounds were welcome and all sights were gay.
With the kind patient trees I had my way,
My eager way. Good trees, unlike to men,
Each journeying year you gave to me again,
And seemed to join me in my rugged play.

Now I am old I seek the grove once more,
To find the trees that were my joy are few—
And they, alack! are old as well as I!
Some leaves are barren that were green before—
But as each year their tops their life renew,
The fruit they bear is nearer to the sky.

Dr. Schumann, though as patient and as careful in his work as a Chinese ivory carver, was possessed at the same time of an extraordinary facility, which was often a source of wonder to his literary friends. He was at his best when manipulating the so-called "set" forms of verse, producing on at least one occasion no fewer than three technically flawless ballads in a single day. Always a lover of the old French forms, he wrote ballades, rondeaux, villanelles and rondels by the score, as he wrote sonnets by the hundred, and always with his characteristic precision and general excellence. No doubt this precision was in the nature of things occasionally a little overdone, but on the other hand the final product was often a thing of pure music and beauty. He wrote for the sheer love of writing, and thereby produced effects that could not have been produced in any other way. The following ballade, for example, with all its artifice, could not have been written for the sake of the lines alone:

THE SONG THAT I SHALL NEVER SING

When twilight's purples pass to gray
And stars emerge in majesty,
When Night's dim fingers close the day
And all is hush and ecstasy—
From the fond homes of memory,
In immemorial murmuring,
Supreme, illusive, comes to me
The song that I shall never sing.

The words allure, delude, delay,
Kiss, captivate, combine, agree,
Flash, quiver, tantalize and play,
Then soar in matchless harmony:
I thrill with unconjectured glee
To catch the final faultless ring—
When sudden fades, and utterly,
The song that I shall never sing.

The voice of bird from budding spray,
When winter dies by spring's decree—
The flush and perfume of the May,
Which quickens meadow, field and tree—
Vague throbs of far-heard melody,
The perfect poise of perfect wing,
Are hints of what might chance to be
The song that I shall never sing.

ENVOY

Friend, I would give all else for fee,
If by the forfeit I could bring
To my poor brain the power to free
The song that I shall never sing.

Although this poet never strove to any great extent for publicity, and may never have given the subject much thought, it is not at all impossible that time, with his odd revenges, may give to Schumann's name a place above many that are today more conspicuous and reverberating.

ON MY "NEW ENGLAND" SONNET

Having read Mr. Darling's vigorous letter and still more vigorous poem in the *Journal* of last week, I find myself constrained to ask for a small amount of space in which to say a few words of explanation. If Mr. Darling will be good enough to give my unfortunate sonnet one more reading, and if he will observe that Intolerance, used ironically, is the subject of the first sentence ("Intolerance born where the wind, etc.") he will see that the whole thing is a satirical attack not upon New England, but upon the same patronizing pagans whom he flays with such vehemence in his own poem. As a matter of fact, I cannot quite see how the first eight lines of my sonnet are to be regarded as even intelligible if read in any other way than as an oblique attack upon all those who are forever throwing dead cats at New England for its alleged emotional and moral frigidity. As for the last six lines, I should suppose that the deliberate insertion of "It seems" would be enough to indicate the key in which they are written. Apparently Mr. Darling has fallen into the not uncommon error of seizing upon certain words and phrases without pausing to consider just why and how they are used.

Interpretation of one's own irony is always a little distressing, yet in this instance, it appears to be rather necessary. If this leaves Mr. Darling still in doubt, it may be assumed that I have written an unusually bad sonnet — which is quite possible.

MACDOWELL'S LEGACY TO ART

Now and then something happens in this contradictory and still enigmatic nation of ours to dislocate a rather firmly fixed notion that we are primarily, if not inevitably, an unclassified conglomerate of materialists and money-worshipers, condescending once in a while to give an hour or two to something higher when our doing so doesn't interfere with our business. We are surely much more and much better than that, and we have risen to many occasions in the past to prove it; and perhaps no better proof of our latent idealism—if we must insist upon giving it some sort of apologetic name—has recently made itself evident than "The *Pictorial Review's* $5,000 Annual Achievement Award for the Year 1923," which has just been conferred upon Mrs. Edward MacDowell,

> for the American woman who makes the most distinctive achievement, through individual effort, in the field of art, industry, literature, music, the drama, education, science or sociology.

The objects of this award are given as three:

> First, to bring to the attention of America and of the rest of the world the creative work of our active woman of today; second, to make it possible for at least one of these women to enjoy a period of relaxation

or a period of concentrated effort (Mrs. MacDowell has enjoyed the last named sort of period for about seventeen years); third, to find and present to the public intimate stories of the life and work of the great women of our day.

In this instance the award may be said to have been made for Mrs. MacDowell's achievement in the fields of art, literature, music and the drama—which means, more comprehensively speaking, in the field of the fine arts. For the Edward MacDowell Association (popularly known as the MacDowell Colony) has been established in Peterborough, N. H., almost wholly through Mrs. MacDowell's personal efforts, and for the purpose of giving to creative workers in all the arts an opportunity to pursue, at a moderate expense, and with none of the difficulties and distractions of the city, the work for which they have proved themselves best fitted in order to make their most logical and important contribution to a world that is not likely to wait any too long for the fulfillment of even the most flaming genius.

For seventeen years Mrs. MacDowell, in the face of almost every conceivable difficulty and misunderstanding, has labored to make of the colony—we may as well call it that—the thing that it is, and now has the satisfaction of seeing thirty buildings where there were three, and 600 acres of land where there were about sixty. All this has involved great labor, an even greater faith, and in the circumstances a relatively great expense; and the time has come when few, if any, new buildings need be added for the fulfillment of the late Edward MacDowell's dream for the furtherance of American art. What is really needed, and needed at once, is an endowment fund of about $300,000. This sum would solve every problem; and as sums go nowadays it is surely not a large one. It is so far from large that 300 people contributing $1,000 each or 1,000 people contributing $300, each, would do the thing at once.

The chief obstacle in the way of raising this relatively small amount appears to be the difficulty in "getting over" the scope, purpose and appearance of the place to those who have not seen it. Almost every person of means who has worked there (the possession of money or the lack of it has nothing whatever to do with the matter), and many who have merely seen the place, have been impelled through sheer conviction of having seen something sound, sincere and lasting to leave behind them a substantial and in several instances a munificent testimony of appreciation.

Generally speaking, the financial policy of the MacDowell Colony is that of a university—the vital difference consisting in the fact that the residents of the colony have not only gone through their "university" but have already attained to at least a considerable degree of distinction. Except in a few frankly experimental instances, no composer, writer, painter or sculptor has been admitted without a significant record of achievement behind him. With an average attendance of from twenty to twenty-five workers in the various arts, it would be absurd even to dream of all coming to eminence, but it is not in the least absurd to dream of a considerable number of them as important contributors to our cultural development. Men of genius or of high talent are not like island peaks that rise alone somewhere from a sea of incompetence. Some rise higher than others, but where there are a few of the higher sort there are scores, if not hundreds, of a lower sort—yet perhaps just as significant. The high and the low together show what has been going on underneath. For a material analogy it might be better to go to the trees in a forest, or, better still, to the flowers in a cultivated garden. The trees in the forest are at least subject to conditions that might be made more favorable through human agency, whereas with the flowers in the garden (once granting that some of them are inherently fitted for a finer and higher and more peculiar development than the others) the human influence is almost everything. Master trees, master flowers and master men are all rare in the best of circumstances, but none of us will ever know how many have been thwarted in their attempt to grow in the wrong soil or to forge a way through contemporary indifference by means of weapons and impulses that were shaped and inherited for entirely different ends.

In the case of an artist of anything like the first order, assuming that he have any chance at all, I am inclined to believe that something of the first order will contrive somehow to find a way out of him—even though it be only a tragic fragment or so, like one or two by Thomas Hood. But unless we choose to fold our hands and assume the attitude of an uncompromising fatalism that is altogether antipathetic to what the late Barrett Wendell would have called the American "temper," we cannot reasonably or even rationally assume that that genius and talent will take care of themselves like the birds and the fishes, or that environment and opportunity are to be discountenanced or dismissed. No doubt it is good for all creators, in all lines of endeavor, to overcome a considerable number of exasperating obstacles, and to profit moderately by the beneficent torture of deferred hopes, but these traditional blessings may be overdone. Wagner, for example, may have made a great deal of epistolary noise over his hardships and disappointments, and yet one wonders what sort of Wagner we should have today but for the loyalty of his friends—notably that of the long-suffering and magnanimous Liszt and the peculiar King Ludwig of Bavaria. Beethoven suffered all manner of insults from his inferiors (not to mention his "superiors"), to die finally, and almost friendless, in a verminous bed. Probably it is better for our detached and exclusive sensibilities that we forget the insults and the vermin when we listen to the Fifth Symphony or to Opus 106, but they were there all the same, and it may not be wholly a soft-headed heresy to believe that they may not have contributed more than two-thirds to the master's ultimate glory. Schubert, working under more leisurely conditions, might well have disciplined an unfailing inspiration which for lack of discipline may be said not infrequently to have failed.

The mere probability that there are no Beethovens or Wagners or Schuberts or Shakespeares alive today does not signify that there are no more to come, or that only geniuses of the first order are valuable and necessary in the social and artistic life of our groping and hungry race. If this were true, we should be living in a drab and barren world, indeed; and it is to make the world less drab and less barren that the MacDowell Colony has existed and persisted for seventeen years, and will, it is to be hoped, exist indefinitely. An artist in any field, with something really to say, can say and do more in four months of the quiet and seclusion it affords than in four years of hand to mouth uncertainty and constant interruption and unrest. It was not my intention to bring anything personal into this brief and inadequate article—but I can see no particular reason for not saying in conclusion that I have written it as one who has experienced both these aforesaid conditions. However much or little my work may be worth, whatever remnant of it may or may not for a time survive, the greater part of it owes its existence to the seclusion of the MacDowell Colony in the New Hampshire woods. And what is true in my experience is true in that of many others who will agree with me in all that I have said—and more.

A NOTE ON MYRON B. BENTON
(1834-1902)

Like many an unassuming man before him, the late Myron B. Benton may be said to have been predestined to a sort of casual immortality. If we could know the whole truth of the matter, perhaps we should know to our surprise and possible discomfiture that all so called earthly immortality, which is only a long name for long remembrance, is casual or accidental, or what you will. At any rate, we all know that many who have failed in their special attempt have worked harder and longer than many who have attained to that uncertain and often unsatisfying thing called success; and perhaps it is better for our vanity and our peace of mind that most of us do not waste much of our time in wondering whether a man is born to be what he is, or whether it is he that makes himself what he is. It may be the kind illusion of a special providence that permits most of us, at least to a considerable extent, to assume the latter inference to be true, or it may be nothing of the sort.

Whatever the truth may be, it is fairly obvious that Mr. Benton, to whom Henry David Thoreau sent the last letter that he ever wrote (or rather dictated), was not much given to worrying about the universe. Like Margaret Fuller, he "accepted" it; and it is evident that he did so without her preliminary reluctance and hesitation. He not only accepted it, but approved of it so intensely as to exclaim at the end of one of his poems, "O God, is there another world so sweet!"

Thoreau, with his famous "one world at a time," just before he died, would hardly have gone so far as that.

From all that one can gather concerning Mr. Benton's mind and character from his own words and from those of his friends—among whom were his well known cousin Joel Benton, John Burroughs, Moncure D. Conway, Richard Henry Stoddard, and apparently almost every one else who had the good fortune to know him—he must have been prëeminently the sort of being whom we call in homely parlance "a rare soul," and a true son of the earth in the very best sense. Referring to himself and to his antecedents, he writes to a friend that "we have hugged the soil close—an unbroken line of farmers,—how far back in England green and old I do not know, but doubtless a long way. The bucolic association has permeated the very blood, and I feel it in every heartbeat." It is impossible to detect from collected evidence anything resembling a real fault in this man, though it is with no disrespect or easy patronage that one finds it impossible to say the same of his poems—which, while wholesome and not too pretentious, are not especially distinctive or exciting. They are the work of a cultivated man who wrote verses because he enjoyed writing them. The man himself was his most important contribution to the world that he loved so much, and there is something singularly fitting in his receipt of Thoreau's last letter.

With the shadow of death so near to him, it is not probable that Thoreau would have felt himself impelled to go to the trouble of writing so kindly and so intimately to a total stranger if he had not discovered and appreciated in the stranger's letter a mingled quality of sincerity and distinction that called even from a dying man for more than a passing respect and attention. Mr. Benton's letter, of which a part is here presented, while properly earnest and appreciative, is in no sense fulsome or extravagant. His words are simply and plainly sincere; and Thoreau, still obscure and still patronized as an "odd stick" by many who should have known better, realized that a true and earnest voice had come to him out of the unknown, and that somewhere there was one who knew. To a dying man of genius, confident of his achievement but almost unrecognized for what he really was, such a tribute from a stranger must have meant a great deal; and his reply —pathetic, though not in any sense complaining—must have meant a great deal more to its far more obscure and unassuming recipient. Perhaps Thoreau should not be referred to as assuming, yet he did know pretty well what he was doing and made no superfluous profession of modesty about it. In fact, he may be said to have come as near to knowing what he was doing as any writer that ever lived.

Probably Mr. Benton, on the other hand, had no very definite notions as to the importance of his less ambitious performances, and apparently did not worry much more about his future fame than he did about the universe. With all his talents, which were by no means inconsiderable, his fate might still be that of a happily-earned obscurity, but for his poignant and unique letter from Thoreau and for his long and intimate correspondence with John Burroughs. To say that Myron Benton was a man of genius would be a false compliment. It would be more to the point to say that he represented the best and highest type of character that makes this world worth living in. Whatever we choose to call him, his name will have to endure for a long time to come,—long after many that are now far more familiar are forgotten.

TRIBUTE TO THEODORE ROOSEVELT

While my personal acquaintance with Colonel Roosevelt may be described as rather slight, his wholly unsuspected appreciation of my work assumed a form that gave me a somewhat unusual acquaintance with certain of his methods, in circumstances that would hardly be familiar to the people at large. It is, therefore, with great pleasure, and with much gratitude, that I record an occurrence which in a life like his may not unlikely have been measured as casual and incidental. But whatever it may have been to him, there was nothing casual or incidental about it so far as I was concerned—especially as it happened at a time when my secular affairs were in a condition that might conservatively have been defined as a little more than precarious and something less than desperate.

But President Roosevelt knew nothing about me or my affairs when a copy of one of my books first found its way into his hands, and for some reason or other not only attracted his fancy, but awoke in him a curiosity as to the sort of being who had written it. Consequently, as I was to learn later, he went promptly out of his official way to write a few letters of inquiry, including one to the late Richard Watson Gilder, then editor of the *Century Magazine,* from whom he obtained a former New York address of mine at a time when I was trying to write advertisements in Boston for a man who was of the best, even though his advertisements were not. In addition to transmitting an expired address, Mr. Gilder was able also to give the President a considerable amount of information as to my previous and present condition of servitude, and apparently to encourage him in his belief that my poetry was not altogether deplorable or joyous. There were some strange and reprehensible derelicts in that book of mine; and the stranger and more reprehensible they were, the better the President seemed to like them—probably because they were not fundamentally vicious.

The somewhat prevalent and wholly foolish notion that Colonel Roosevelt was tolerant only, or mainly, of biceps and sunshine was clearly disproved in his disinterested and business-like pursuit of the person who was responsible for this book just mentioned—a book in which the characters, taken together, are of a certainty neither strenuous nor sunny. They may be interesting, and I hope they are, but I am pretty certain that their combined example would lead one sooner to the devil than to the White House. But as Colonel Roosevelt was manifestly in no danger of going to the devil, and was already in the White House, probably he felt himself to be immune from any contagion of insufficiency and general uselessness to which some of my eccentric citizens may have exposed him. At any rate, he remembered me and finally tracked me to my dingy room in Boston; and in a few days was able to offer me a position in the New York Custom House. And for that attention to a total stranger—an attention that was rewarded, I fear, with varying degrees of diligence and efficiency—I am happy too, owing to Colonel Roosevelt an increasing indebtedness of gratitude for which there is unhappily no tangible return. The best and only acknowledgment that I can make of a most unusual act on the part of a most unusual man must apparently be told only in my gratefulness and in a few inadequate words.

A TRIBUTE TO FRANKLIN L. SCHENCK

The funeral of the late Franklin L. Schenck at East Northport on Wednesday of last week was an impressive illustration of the power that lives in personality and character, as opposed to mere conventional success and worldly possessions. All those who were present must have realized, and perhaps a little more keenly than ever before, that Mr. Schenck was an altogether different man, and that in losing him they were losing something never conceivably to be replaced. There was in the town an atmosphere of spontaneous tribute and affection that somehow made Mr. Schenck's funeral a little different from other funerals, just as Mr. Schenck himself was different from other men.

He was different from other men in many ways, and notably so in his quiet and good natured determination to live his own life in accordance with his own ideals, regardless of what others might say or think. Worldly wealth and social conventions meant no more to him than the dirt under his feet, and in truth not half so much. For the dirt under his feet gave his flowers and his vegetables an opportunity to grow and his chickens an opportunity to scratch; as his flowers and his vegetables and his chickens were for Mr. Schenck far more significant and important than all the fame for which he cared so little, and all the money for which he cared nothing. With a few dollars to keep him alive, any further attention to economics would have been to him a waste of life and a martyrdom; and with his opportunity to paint when he pleased, any attempt to make his methods conform to those of any prevailing temporary style would have been to him an insult to his conscience and to his art. All he asked of life was the privilege to be himself, knowing well that in doing so he was making his best and proper contribution to the world. Compromise would have killed him. He could no more have compromised, even if he tried, than he could have done an evil act or have harbored an evil wish. It is my honest belief that he never wished anything but good to any human being. If there were a few who may have misjudged him for his informalities and eccentricities, he knew them better than they knew themselves and wished them well. All those who really knew the man must have loved him, there was nothing else for them to do. The world is better for his having lived in it — which is perhaps as much as will be said of many of us, and perhaps a little more, when our houses are left empty and our memories are left to flourish or dwindle as they may. The dead go fast, the saying is, but Franklin Schenck will go slowly, very slowly from the place where he is so much alive.

Men like Franklin Schenck are in a sense their own monuments, yet it is pleasant to know that he has another monument, and a beautiful one, in the form of a permanent exhibition of his best paintings on the walls of the Brooklyn Chamber of Commerce.

FRANKLIN SCHENCK
(1856-1927)

One would hardly suspect from the evidence of Franklin Schenck's work that he, the predestined poet and idealist, was in his earlier life a pupil, and even a "favorite" pupil, of the late Thomas Eakins, the great realist. But he was exactly that, and quotation marks are therefore unnecessary; and the statement is significant, if only as an illustration of the broad-mindedness of the dreamer.

But all this was long ago. Most of these pictures now placed on exhibition were painted during the last twenty years of the artist's life, many of them in his small house at East Northport, Long Island, where he died a year ago. He painted always in his own way, convinced that his way was for him the only way — a conviction in which he was indubitably right.

Beauty and genius were the two things that he looked for in a work of art, and he was always ready to welcome and enjoy them even in the work of those whose methods and tenets were farthest from his. In his own work there is a combination of beauty and genius which becomes the more apparent with a more familiar acquaintance; and in these quiet pictures there is a quality that is likely to outlive that of many which may make a more obvious appeal and perhaps a more obvious noise.

INTRODUCTION TO *THE LETTERS OF THOMAS SERGEANT PERRY*

Anyone who had the privilege of knowing personally the subject of this volume will be glad to find him again in these few letters of his which have been selected from the many hundreds that he wrote; and those who did not know him will find in them at least a reflection of a personality that was as engaging as it was unusual, as facetious as it was ferocious, and as amiable as it was annihilating. He was not always engaging or facetious or amiable, but even in his depressions and indignations he was always distinguished. After the surrender of Cervera at Santiago, an American officer is reported to have said, "It is asking a great deal of any man to climb aboard an enemy's battleship with nothing but his sword and his underclothes to distinguish him, and still look like an admiral, but Cervera did it." Thomas Sergeant Perry could have done it, if he had been an admiral—or, like his illustrious ancestor, a commodore.

But with all his dignity and intelligence, and with all his youthful activity as a boatman and a swimmer, one doubts if he would have been a happy admiral, or commodore, or if in later life he would have been altogether at ease or at home on the ocean. He must have admired the ocean, as he admired all sublime and magnificent things, and he had been over it to a considerable extent; yet one suspects that, like Lucretius, he found it on the whole more attractive and more impressive when studied comfortably from the shore. On land he was an indomitable walker and tennis-player and bicycle-rider, and yet he was not, in any proper way of speaking, a man of action. He was a man of books. He liked physical exercise, and always took good care of the remarkable body with which he was born, and with which, fortunately, he never had much trouble until old age came upon him, rather swiftly and kindly, and with far less pain than is usually alloted for mortals before their release. But he was born a man of books, and a man of books he lived and died.

He was a great reader, a great friend, and a great gentleman. Whether or not he might have been a great writer is more than one can say, for he never took the trouble to find out. He was an accomplished writer always, or when he chose to be one, and perhaps he was content to let it go at that. He left mostly to others the pangs and pleasures of literary creation, holding himself always in readiness to enjoy or to execrate the result. Alone in his study, with a troublesome world forgotten and out of his way, he made one think sometimes of an experienced and insatiable spider—beneficent or terrible, as the case might be—waiting there to suck the living juice, if he found it, of anything literary that might fly into his clutches. A taste, and often a glance, was enough to tell him the quality of his prey. A native sophistication, long disciplined, served as a protection against the ephemeral and the unsubstantial. For one who read so much, and along so many lines, he lost an incredibly small amount of time in experimenting with mistakes or in getting himself involved in voluminous and able works that might command his respect without arousing his interest. Once in a while, however, he would read such a work, and he would sigh with a scholar's recognition of so much toil and learning gone to the making of so little that was alive. Such books were monuments, perhaps, but to him it was almost a personal sorrow that a writer should be at the same time so competent and so hard to read. But they were books, all the same; they were worthy and admirable books, and were not to be dismissed with levity or with disrespect. They were like some worthy and admirable people whom he would rather not have in the house.

There is no careless exaggeration in saying that books to him were like people. Books to him were living things, and a world without them would have been, in his estimation, as complete an inferno as the most diabolical of medieval minds could have imagined for the damnedest of heretics. Books were the next thing to the breath of life to him, and without them the breath of life itself would have been, so far as he was concerned, a phenomenon hardly worthy of investigation, and surely not one to be prolonged. He regarded life frankly, and without complaint or criticism, as a mystery so tragic and bewildering as to be beyond all human comprehension or conjecture, and had therefore not much veneration for metaphysical philosophers. "Philosophy," he said one day, with all possible cheerfulness, "is at its best and highest the attempt of someone to tell me what he doesn't know." He always respected, on the other hand, the religious convictions of his friends, though it would be a false loyalty to pretend that he gave much thought to them, or that he attached to them any particular significance beyond the comfort that others might find in them. In the meantime he estimated character and conduct far beyond accomplishment or glory, and acknowledged only with sorrow and reluctance that a great genius was not always a great man. Sometimes, again, his prejudices, which were active and incurable, may have blinded or deafened him to the enjoyment of beauty that he would not see or hear. He had, for example, so violent a dislike for Wagner as a man that he would listen to his music only under compulsion. He would gladly have found pretty much the same tom-cats and valerian in parts of the *Ring* and in *Tristan* that the late Dr. Max Nordau succeeded once in finding there. But his prejudices, though violent and expensive, as prejudices are likely to be, were for the most part harmless, and were perhaps more picturesque than important. His really righteous indignations came from the depths of his sincerity and his experience.

Although an aristocrat by birth and instinct and environment, he was far more democratic in his feelings and interests than were most of the professional proletarians who might have regarded him as one of the last of the Boston Brahmins, or as an exclusive conservative clinging sadly to the crumbling remnants of the old order. But he was too energetic and too sensible for that. He knew, like many others, that the Great War had carried away with it the world that he had known, and in which he had best belonged; he knew also that time was at his heels, and that the new world would somehow take care of itself without him. He was undoubtedly more at home with his Victorian memories than with his twentieth century questionings and apprehensions—which occupied but a small part of his time. The new order, or disorder, might destroy the landscape, along with other familiar things that he had liked, but it could not destroy his books—a dispensation for which he was snugly thankful. It could even produce new books that he could read and enjoy. Though nurtured on the classics, and still on easy terms with his Latin and Greek, he surprised himself and all his friends in his later years by learning Russian—not the alphabet and how-do-you-do, but the whole formidable language—and in reading almost everything in Russian that could be called literature. His naturally realistic, or rationalistic, mind found at last in the plays and tales of Chekov something for which he had been always looking, and he admired them beyond measure for their competence and honesty, and for their avoidance of any attempt to blur man's finite vision with misty glimmerings of the infinite. When I told him once that it was this very quality in Chekov that kept him from being really great, he agreed with me, rather to my surprise, and continued, naturally and rightly, in his praise of *The Three Sisters.*

If I have called him—by implication, at least—a Victorian, I have done so with a complete conviction that he would have no sort of objection. For that, with his temperament and his intellectual heritage, he could not very well have been anything else. He flayed America, but he remained always an American at heart. He loved England, and the English tradition, but he had little patience with anything that savored of Anglomania—as he revealed one day to an earnest medievalist who deplored the encroachments of time and change, and especially the formation of republics. "Perry," he said, "there are times when I yearn to be a subject." — "What's the matter?" said Perry. "Aren't you contented with being an object?"—He was not often so abrupt or so incisive as that. He may have eaten something that he should not have eaten, or he may have had a twinge of gout. With a sense of humor that was always comprehensive, he would say that his ancestors had all the fun, leaving for him a few fingers that should have been theirs. Fortunately it was only an occasional visitor, and did not interfere with his reading of Chekov, or with his pleasure in not having to read *Salammbô*—against which remarkable production he maintained an animosity that was as respectful as it was unalterable. "It must be a masterpiece," he would say, "for people say so who should know. There's nothing wrong with it, except that it isn't to be read." And so the matter was settled for ever. He did not have to read a book in order to know that it was not written for him; and his literary prejudices at least, must have robbed him of far less than they spared. He was a life-long friend of Henry James, admiring him both as a writer and as a man; but he found too many words in the later novels, and simply would not read them, even for love; and there would have been no especial sense in his reading them, for he could not possibly have enjoyed them. By that time James had invented a new language, which his old friend had never found time to learn. Perhaps Russian had been enough.

Having read almost everything when he was young, he found difficulty, as he approached old age, in reading any fiction that was not Russian. Novels, generally speaking, were pretty well behind him now, although he read nearly every other sort of book imaginable—excepting philosophy, which he had always eyed askance. Novels mostly wearied him. "If they are true to life," he would say, "they are only depressing. If they are not true to life, they are only silly; and novels are too long anyhow." Granting the general validity of all that, one may still be haunted by a few lingering uncertainties; for while *Madame Bovary* and *The Mayor of Casterbridge* were too long, five volumes of the Letters of X. Doudon, which had a special place of honor in his library, were not long enough; and Professor Moore's two mighty volumes on *Judaism* were apparently just right—as no doubt they are. At any rate, he caressed them with approving hands, and praised them, with no reference to their length, in a way that would surely have been a joy to their learned author, had he been there.

But it must not be inferred from the foregoing remarks that he was always solemn in his later years, for he could approve almost anything that was in its way first rate. He could relish an occasional dash of vulgarity, if it was not cheap, and he could enjoy thoroughly any amount of nonsense that was good nonsense. Always apart from a few prejudices —which on the whole made him only the more human and interesting—his *flair* for the best was all but infallible. He was fastidious, but he was far from being antiquated or ungenerous in his likes and dislikes. Though he clung fondly to the past, he was watchful all the time of what the younger men were doing, here and abroad; and as I have no personal acquaintance with Mr. T. S. Eliot or Mr. Van Wyck Brooks, it will do no harm for me to mention here his lively and especial interest in their work. By way of antithesis, it may also be interesting to know that he got a great deal of satisfaction from the racy vigor of the late William Marion Reedy, and often wished that the best of his editorials might be made available in a book—an enterprise, by the way, that is still possible.

With all his courtesy, his cheerfulness, and his charm, he was, I suppose, in our careless and rather meaningless use of the word, a pessimist. Whatever he was, he was not an optimist. He accepted gracefully his condition as a member of the human race, although he never quite succeeded in discovering any satisfactory reason why such a race should have been called into existence. On the other hand, he was in no sense an atheist. He would have considered atheism ridiculous, if only for its assumption of a knowledge that no human being could possibly possess. Not having inherited or acquired a special interest in the abstract or the mystical, he simply left such questions to others who valued them, thus quietly avoiding what would have been for him a futile controversy over the unknowable. He liked best the things that he could see and feel and get hold of. The substance of things hoped for and the evidence of things not seen may have comforted him somewhat as a rare morsel of intellectual humor, but it could never have sustained him on a long and patient journey through one life to another. He found enough in this life that was mysterious and bewildering, and saw no good reason for exploring or disturbing eternity for an evidence of new uncertainties. He was an incurious agnostic. At the same time he was one of the best and cleanest men that ever lived. Dirt, whether physical or mental, was simply dirt to him, and it was nothing more—except when transmuted by the admixture of an impudent and irresistible genius. He would never have tolerated, for example, any improvement of Rabelais or of Aristophanes, or any of the authentic giants. Greatness might have its own way, but littleness had best be careful. His few attempts to read some of the "dirty little people," as he called them, of to-day, were brief and painful, and his pity for their misguided effort was profound.

For that matter, his sorrow for mankind, and especially for womankind, was also profound, although he never said much about it. His reticences were as incurable as cloudy weather while they lasted, and were quite as misleading. Strangers might readily have supposed that he was "always like that," and so might have been ridiculously mistaken—not to say unfortunate. "Charm" is a word not often applied to men so masculine as he, yet he had it to a degree that might have been, and probably was, sometimes, the despair of women. When he was in the mood, or when he took the trouble, he could make his conversation an art in which he was likely to be challenged by few competitors. When he was not in the mood, he said nothing, or nothing remarkable; and one was left to wonder what was going on in his mind—which, though crotchety sometimes, was surely seldom idle.

There were sorrows in his life, and there must have been the disappointments that are so much of life; and there was one injustice that left a permanent mark upon him. But his native courtesy and poise covered all his pains and his problems pretty thoroughly from the knowledge of other people—though not always. Not always, of course; for then he would not have been human—and he was eminently human. During his later years—which were clouded by a long bereavement to which he seldom referred, and for which nothing more could be done—my talk with him turned one day to the arts in general, and to the heavy penalty so many times exacted by fate for their production. During this talk I happened to mention Tasso in prison, without the manuscript of his great poem, with no knowledge of where it might be, and with no certain knowledge that it was even in existence. At that a complete change came over him. He looked at me with a sort of cold fire in his eyes, and his body and his voice trembled as he spoke: "That simply goes to show," he said, pointing a forefinger at me, "that there is absolutely no limit to what the human heart can endure." A few minutes later he was as cheerful and as genial as ever, and was praising Chekov with possibly a little more than his usual enthusiasm.

He always insisted that he was not a writer, which was a fairly obvious nonsense. If he meant that he was not a great creator—a great poet, a great novelist, or a great what-not—he was probably right; yet if his impulse had been only a little stronger, he might easily have written volumes of brilliant and authoritative criticism, or of almost anything that would have given his intellect and his personality a free range. But there was one insuperable obstacle in the way, and one that he appears never to have striven seriously to overcome. So much writing as all that, and the time necessarily involved, would have interfered seriously with his reading. There were books enough without his, he may have reasoned; and some of them, even some of those by the younger men, were not so bad. And there was always the inexhaustible past.

Considering him in retrospect, and as he was born to be, I see him rather as one of the great appreciators—without whom there would be no great writers, or artists of any sort—than as a dynamic and predestined penman. He enjoyed writing letters, but it is difficult to believe that he really enjoyed the writing of books. If he had enjoyed writing them, he would have written more of them—having every conceivable opportunity. His literary ambitions may never have worried or excited him half so much as they worried and excited his friends. It would not be fantastic or extravagant to believe that the one thing he really cared about and wanted, apart from his family, his friends, and his books, was denied him by a twist of fate that partly concealed itself in the manifold ramifications of academic diplomacy. He would have given the best of himself to younger men with more joy and satisfaction than he would ever have had from the applause of his contemporaries. He might have welcomed fame, if he had found it waiting for him at his door, but he would never have been deceived by it, and would never have gone far from his books and his friends for the sake of its unreliable acquaintance. He must have been conscious of much to give that was not to be given, yet here again he never criticised or complained. Whatever his thoughts or feelings or opinions may have been, he kept them to himself. He was a great gentleman, and a great friend; and his personality was one that was remembered wherever he went, and long after the man himself had vanished. He was not the less valuable and rare for not having had the dictation of his destiny, or for not having made a loud noise with his name.

In the foregoing paragraphs, which are as sincere as they are inadequate, it will be seen that nothing of a biographical nature has been attempted. For an admirable account of his life, the reader is referred to *Thomas Sergeant Perry: A Memoir* (Boston, 1929) by his old friend John T. Morse, Jr. The following letters and selections, which call for little or no editorial illumination, will be found remarkably easy to read—although they are no better, perhaps, than many others that might have been selected.

In acknowledging gratefully my indebtedness to Mrs. Perry and to Miss Margaret Perry for their invaluable assistance in the preparation of this volume, I can only hope that the result may not be too far from what they wished it to be. The letters themselves, I trust, will ensure the evasion of any violent disapproval.

THE ARTHURIAN TRILOGY AND "RABBI BEN EZRA"

In writing *Tristram* I was merely telling a story, using the merest outline of the old legend. Perhaps I should say adapting rather than using. There isn't much for you to write about it except in the way of general criticism. There is no symbolic significance in it, although there is a certain amount in *Merlin* and *Lancelot,* which were suggested by the world war — Camelot representing in a way the going of a world that is now pretty much gone. But possibly these two poems may be read just as well as narrative poems with no inner significance beyond that which is obvious. There is no "philosophy" in my poetry beyond an implication of an ordered universe and a sort of deterministic negation of the general futility that appears to be the basis of "rational" thought. So I suppose you will have to put me down as a mystic, if that means a man who cannot prove all his convictions to be true.

I dislike "Rabbi Ben Ezra" so much as a poem that I haven't read it in something like thirty years, but I should say, not having a very clear memory of it, that its easy optimism is a reflection of temperament rather than of experience and observation.

Those who do me the great honor of reading my books must excuse me from trying to interpret them — an occupation in which I should probably fail.

INTRODUCTORY LETTER TO *WIND IN THE GRASS*

It has been a great pleasure for me to read these poems of yours in manuscript, and its gives me pleasure of another sort to tell you that I find in them the presence of something for which there is no name in the dictionaries.

Whatever it is, it has a quality that is unusual and intangible, and one that makes all the difference between poetry and mere verse. In these poems there are many flashes of a real imagination, by which I mean the imagination that comes apparently from nowhere, and brings with it something that we did not have before

There is no recipe for this sort of thing, and no amount of calling or whistling for it will make it come. I can only say that its presence in these early poems arouses in me a lively sense of curiosity and expectancy, and that it reveals far more than a suggestion of achievement. The thing itself is already here, and it seizes the reader every now and then as he examines what you have done.

This is a great deal for anyone to say of any early book of poems, and I am glad to be able to say it and to call myself, at the same time, / Yours sincerely, / E. A. R.

THE FIRST SEVEN YEARS

Whenever I have occasion to turn the leaves of a rather formidable looking book of mine entitled *Collected Poems,* the sight of a section of it called *The Children of the Night* is likely to make me realize unwillingly, and with an effort, that some of those early poems were written more than forty years ago. In those days time had no special significance for a certain juvenile and incorrigible fisher of words who thought nothing of fishing for two weeks to catch a stanza, or even a line, that he would not throw back into a squirming sea of language where there was every word but the one he wanted. There were strange and iridescent and impossible words that would seize the bait and swallow the hook and all but drag the excited angler in after them, but like that famous catch of Hiawatha's, they were generally not the fish he wanted. He wanted fish that were smooth and shining and subtle, and very much alive, and not too strange; and presently, after long patience and many rejections, they began to bite.

Many of those slippery victims went into the preparation and final accomplishment of innumerable short poems and sonnets that had certainly many faults and at least one merit. For me, at any rate, there was a sort of merit in their not being quite like anything else — or anything that I remembered. But a kindly providence had given me a modicum of common sense that was always reminding me of my age — from sixteen to twenty — and warning me that my somewhat peculiar productions, no matter how radical or different they might be, could not in the nature of things be much more than technical exercises. I had read of John Milton writing "L'Allegro" and "Il Penseroso" at a most annoyingly early age and could only make the best of it, having been told that the English mind matures anywhere from five to ten years earlier than our minds over here. That was a comfort, for I was compelled to acknowledge, and even to myself, that I could not write "L'Allegro" or "Il Penseroso," no matter how hard I might try. It was a concession, but I made it.

It was about my seventeenth year when I became violently excited over the structure and music of English blank verse, and in order to find out a little more about it I made — of all things possible — a metrical translation of Cicero's first oration against Catiline, which we were reading in school. It began well enough, and with no difficulty:

> O Catiline, how long will you abuse
> Our patience?

That was easy, and invited me to go on. If it lacked something of the vindictive resonance that we feel in the Latin, the fault was not in me but in the English language, for which I was not responsible. So I went on with it until the whole diatribe, which is not short, lay before me in a clean copy of impeccable pentameters (I thought then that they were impeccable) which looked at a glance very much as an equal amount of *Paradise Lost* would have looked if I had copied it on the same quality of paper. It may not have been poetry, and probably wasn't, but many portions of it had music and rhythm and an unmistakable presence of what is nowadays called a punch — for which Cicero may possibly deserve some credit. It was written and rewritten with a prodigality of time that only youth can afford, with an elaborately calculated variation of the cæsura, and with a far more laborious devotion than was ever expended on anything that I was supposed to be studying. When this rather unusual bit of minstrelsy was accomplished, and followed by a similar treatment of long passages from Virgil, I had the profound and perilous satisfaction of knowing a great deal more about the articulation and anatomy of English blank verse than I had known before. A few years later I nearly wore myself out one summer over a metrical translation, made from a literal English version furnished by a schoolmate of mine who is now Professor Smith of Amherst College, of the *Antigone* — which has disappeared mysteriously, and I trust for ever. Not that it was altogether bad; it was just one of those juvenile experiments that we would rather not have brought in evidence against us. If ever it should come to light, I hope the finder will heed my solemn request that it shall not be published.

It must have been about the year 1889 when I realized finally, and not without a justifiable uncertainty as to how the thing was to be done, that I was doomed, or elected, or sentenced for life, to the writing of poetry. There was nothing else that interested me, and I was rational enough to keep the grisly secret to myself. Perhaps I was afraid of being arrested; perhaps I was afraid that my father and mother, the best and kindest of parents, would have had my head examined if they had known what was going on inside it. They knew already that I was unpractical, and indifferent — to say it mildly — to any of the world's reputable pursuits, and they knew that I was inordinately addicted to reading the somewhat unusual amount of poetry that was in the house; but they did not know the worst. My father died without suspecting it; my mother did not live to see printed evidence of it — which, while it would have interested her intensely, might still have given her reason to see more darkly than ever, in her affectionate imagination, a prospect that was dark enough even for me whenever I strained my mind's eye for the sight of more than a little of it at a time. For something told me at an early age, long before there was any material reason for worry, that they whose lives are to be chronically hazardous and uncertain should take only short views ahead. Before the family fortune, such as it was, went to smash, I could see it going and could see myself setting out alone on what was inevitably to be a long and foggy voyage. The prospect was interesting, if it was not altogether reassuring.

But I was not much occupied then with the future, which must somehow or other, so far as I was concerned, fulfil itself in its own way. I was chiefly occupied with the composition of short poems and sonnets, which I would read to my old friend and neighbor, Dr. A. T. Schumann, who was himself a prolific writer of sonnets, ballades and rondeaus, and a master of poetic technique. As I shall never know the extent of my indebtedness to his interest and belief in my work, or to my unconscious absorption of his technical enthusiasm, I am glad for this obvious opportunity to acknowledge a debt that I cannot even estimate. Perhaps I was not quite veracious in saying a moment ago that my poetic aspirations and determinations were exclusively a matter of my own knowledge, for the doctor must have known, with his knowledge of humanity and human frailty, the dangerous fate that was before me. In fact, he told me once that I should have to write poetry or starve, and that I might do both — although he did not believe that I should starve, or not exactly. That was encouraging, and I have never forgotten it. If he had cared as much about "the numerous ills inwoven with our frame" as he did about the metrical defects and tonal shortcomings of the major and minor English poets, he would surely have been a most remarkable doctor; as it was, I am sure that he was one of the most remarkable metrical technicians that ever lived, and an invaluable friend to me in those years of apprenticeship when time, as a commodity to be measured and respected, did not exist. There were such things as hours and days and weeks on clocks and calendars, but it made no difference to me how few or many of them went to my getting a few lines to go as as I wanted them to go. It was no uncommon performance of mine to write a sonnet in twenty minutes or half an hour, and work over it for twenty days — an expenditure of life for which the doctor could not conscientiously reproach me. One afternoon I found him in his office fairly swelling with triumph and satisfaction, having straightened out a refractory line of his that had been bothering him for two years. All this may have have been bad for the practice of medicine, but apparently it was a part of his fate, and of mine.

After two years at Harvard College (1891-1893) where I made several good friends, I returned to my home in Gardiner, Maine, and worked steadily at my unaccredited profession until 1897, when I went to New York. Sometimes I wondered what my friends and neighbors thought of me, but as it could make no manner of difference to me what they thought, there was nothing for me to do but to go on filing and fitting words until I had words enough to make a book. For three years I sent my wares incessantly to every reputable monthly and weekly periodical in the country—there were not so many in those days as there are now—and invariably got them back, or all but a few that were accepted by some of the less prominent publications or now and then by a newspaper. My collection of rejection slips must have been one of the largest and most comprehensive in literary history, with innumerable duplicates. One sonnet, "The Clerks," having gone the rounds with many others, was sent finally to the New York *Sun,* and was promptly returned with a piece of white paper on which was written with a blue pencil, "Unavailable. Paul Dana." I am surprised and puzzled to this day that Mr. Dana should have gone to that trouble when he might have had a neat pile of printed slips at his elbow. He may have used them all in returning other sonnets.

Whether or not it was the return of "The Clerks" from the *Sun* that started and set going some new wheels in my emotional machinery is more than I can say at this time. But something set them going, and their persistence assured me at last that there would be no use or sense in any further attempt to make my work known to the public through the periodical press. I was not conscious of analyzing my feelings at the time, but a retrospective consideration of them compels me to suspect myself of being quietly and thoroughly disgusted. I hope it was not so bad as that, but probably it was. At any rate, I made a selection of about forty poems from everything that I had written during the past six or seven years and made a small book of them, reasoning prematurely and wildly that publishers might find something in them that editors had overlooked. But a few experimental attacks in their direction only brought the manuscript back to me with a speed that would be remarkable with even our present aerial facilities. There was something wrong somewhere, and as I was still confident that the poems had nothing worse than a new idiom to condemn them, the fault must be somewhere else. By degrees I began to realize that those well-typed and harmless looking verses of mine might as well be written, so far as possible attention or interest on the part of editors and publishers was concerned, in the language of the Senegambians.

> I did not think that I should find them there
> When I came back again

was evidently too much: and not only for Mr. Dana, but for the traditional sensibilities of editors in general.

There was nothing left, so far as I could see, but to print the unwelcome little volume at my own expense, and to let it find its way to recognition or to oblivion as it might. With an obstinate confidence that somehow strengthened itself with each new rebuff, I was unable to foresee oblivion for the poems, though I could foresee too surely a long and obscure journey for them before they should have more than a small number of friends. Fortunately for me, a few really responsive and intelligent readers were all that I should expect or require for some years to come, but I wanted those few readers badly, and knew well enough that I was going to have them. So it was with no feeling of humiliation or surrender that I sent the manuscript to the Riverside Press, from which highly respectable establishment I received in due time three hundred copies of an inconspicuous blue-covered little pamphlet, which I had named, rather arbitrarily, from the first and the last poem: *The Torrent and The Night Before.* The entire edition cost me fifty-two dollars, which I am told is appreciably less than one pays today for a single copy. I am naturally a well-wishing person, and not in the least vindictive; yet sometimes I have wished that all surviving editors and publishers who pointed a cold nose at those early poems might find themselves afflicted with a collector's frenzy for the possession of a copy of that first book of mine published in 1896. My constructive imagination would be mean enough to enjoy the sight of them signing cheques for it.

When my three hundred copies arrived (or three hundred and twelve to be exact) I knew that something important had happened to me. It never occurred to my confident enthusiasm that their arrival, or their existence, might not be important to anybody else, and it was therefore with an untroubled zeal that I began to send them out into the world — more of them to periodicals for possible critical notice, and to strangers who were known to me only by reputation. Perhaps thirty or forty of them went to friends and acquaintances, but the most of them went, as they were intended to go, unsolicited and unannounced into the unknown. Only a few of them—possibly ten or twelve—failed in drawing from its recipient some sort of response. Considering its unimpressive appearance as a publication and the complete obscurity of its origin, it was received generally with a respect and an enthusiasm that was gratifying, and was all that I needed to keep me going through the years of obscurity and material uncertainty that were so definitely before me. My incurable belief in what I was doing made me indifferent alike to hostility or neglect. There was far more neglect than hostility, as a matter of fact, although now and then a protesting voice would be heard saying something that was not especially complimentary or true. One critic took refuge in paraphrase, merely wishing in print that my poetry might be sent to the bourne from which no poetry returns.

I may say in conclusion, and in reply to several who have asked for information on the subject, that I have no means of knowing how many copies of *The Torrent* are now in existence. Considering the few that have come up for sale, perhaps it may be safe to assume that of the original three hundred, something like half that number may have been lost or destroyed. Thirty-four years may be considered a fairly long life for an obscure pamphlet, and especially for a pamphlet of unorthodox poetry by an unknown writer who could find no publisher for it but himself.

In 1897 most of these poems, along with a number of new ones, were published under the title of *The Children of the Night.*

FOR HARRIET MOODY'S COOK BOOK

We should all take off our hats, and we might even consider the possibility of getting down on our knees, in the presence of a good cook. For without good cooks there would be no good food; and without good food there would not be many good people; and without a considerable number of good people, with good digestions and dispositions, this world of ours would be a terrible place. It would be so bad that many of us would refuse to live in it, and would gladly run the risk of any additional damnation for the privilege of getting out of it. These words may seem at first a little violent and exaggerated, but I believe that after a solemn and open minded consideration of their significance, they will be seen as only truthful and temperate. If anyone who reads them should be condemned to the prospect of eating for the rest of his life the equivalent of the worst cookery that he has ever encountered, he would begin at once to be glad for the years that are behind him, and to have glimmerings of a new eschatology.

I have an adequate and familiar name for the few fanatical enthusiasts who insist that we can make ourselves believe that we have the digestive machinery of our alleged arboreal ancestors, and that we can make ourselves useful and happy on a diet of raw fruits and vegetables and nuts. Such a statement may be interesting, and may have a certain economic appeal, but it has the paralysing disadvantage of being a lie. There is no royal road or short cut to learning, or to science, or to art, or the achievement of a good dinner. A good dinner cannot be pulled out of the ground, or knocked on the head, or caught with a hook, or shaken from a tree. It is true that we may live and thrive on bread and milk, and it is true that most of us do nothing of the sort. If we were to be sentenced to such a diet, we should have a right to ask for good bread; and good bread does not just happen. Cooks are greater kings, for without cooks the kings would not be very well, and there might be nothing better for them than to make the best of sorrow, and to wait with the rest of us for the end.

ON THE MEANING OF LIFE

I have delayed my acknowledgement of your letter only for the lack of anything especially profound or valuable to say in reply to it. I told a philosopher once that all the other philosophers would have to go out of business if one of them should happen to discover the truth; and now you say, or imply, in your letter that the truth has been discovered, and that we are only the worse off, if possible, for the discovery. This is naturally a cause of some chagrin and humiliation for me, for I had heard nothing about it. It is true that we have acquired a great deal of material knowledge in recent years, but so far as knowledge of the truth itself is concerned, I cannot see that we are any nearer to it now than our less imaginative ancestors were when they cracked each others' skulls with stone hatchets, or that we know any more than they knew of what happened to the soul that escaped in the process. It is easy, and just now rather fashionable, to say that there is no soul, but we do not know whether there is a soul or not. If a man is a materialist, or a mechanist, or whatever he likes to call himself, I can see for him no escape from belief in a futility so prolonged and complicated and diabolical and preposterous as to be worse than absurd; and as I do not know that such a tragic absurdity is not a fact, I can only know my native inability to believe that it is one. There is nothing in the thought of annihilation that frightens me; for it would be, at the worst, nothing more terrible than going to sleep at the end of a long day, whether a pleasant or a painful one, or both. But if life is only what it appears to be, no amount of improvement or enlightenment will ever compensate or atone for what it has inflicted and endured in ages past, or for what it is inflicting and enduring today . . . There is apparently not much that anyone can do about it except to follow his own light—which may or may not be the light of an *ignis fatuus* in a swamp. The cocksureness of the modern "mechanist" means nothing to me; and I doubt if it means any more to him when he pauses really to think. His position is not entirely unlike that of an intrepid explorer standing on a promontory in a fog, looking through the newest thing in the way of glasses for an ocean that he cannot see, and shouting to his mechanistic friends behind him that he has found the end of the world.

These remarks, which to some readers might seem a little severe, are more the result of observation and reflection than of personal discomfort or dissatisfaction. As lives go, my own life would be called, and properly, a rather fortunate one.

VACHEL LINDSAY

It is easy, in one way, to give to Vachel Lindsay his place; and in another way it is extremely difficult, and at present probably impossible, to do anything of the sort. It is easy, for example, to say that his most characteristic work is utterly unlike the work of any other poet, living or dead. But saying that is saying only what everyone knows already, and does not need to be told again.

On the other hand, it is far from easy to say how large or

lofty a place may sometime be assigned to him, or to his contemporaries, by a posterity that in all probability will not be so patient or so lenient with literature as posterity has been in the past — which may not be saying much for posterity. Time and distance will be required for anything like a valid estimate of the man, or of his contribution to American letters. There was never before, in this or in any country, so peculiar and apparently so triumphant a combination of the troubadour and the evangelist. There was never a minstrel more sincere and uncompromising in his will to wander and to sing, and to sing always in his own way. The greatest part of his work may be forgotten, as the greater part of most men's work will be forgotten, but in the best of Lindsay there appears to exist a nameless quality that vanished cave-dwellers would have understood, and that unborn sophisticates will accept.

THOMAS SERGEANT PERRY

PERRY, THOMAS SERGEANT (Jan. 23, 1845-May 7, 1928), author, scholar, and educator, was born at Newport, R. I. His father, Christopher Grant Perry, was the son of Oliver Hazard Perry, of Lake Erie fame, whose brother, Commodore Matthew Calbraith Perry, became equally famous because of his negotiations with Japan. His mother was Frances Sergeant, of Philadelphia, and on her side he was, by direct descent, the great-great-grandson of Benjamin Franklin, whose facial characteristics he inherited to a degree that was frequently recognized. His early education was at private schools. At the age of sixteen and a half he entered Harvard College, graduating with the class of 1866.

After graduation he went to Europe for further study, with the intention of returning to a position for life at Harvard as a tutor in French and German. After holding this position from 1868 to 1872, however, he relinquished it and became associated for a time with the *North American Review*. Returning to Harvard in 1877 as instructor in English, he remained there for five years. In 1874 he was married to Lilla

Cabot, daughter of Dr. Samuel Cabot of Boston, and soon became an adopted Bostonian. As a lecturer he was notably popular. A volume of his lectures, *English Literature of the Eighteenth Century* (1883), is widely known and read. For several years, at home and abroad, he was engaged in an active literary life. In 1882 he published *The Life and Letters of Francis Lieber,* which was issued also in a German translation; in 1885 *From Opiz to Lessing* appeared. In 1887 he published a small volume in a lighter vein, *The Evolution of the Snob,* which is not, however, so trivial as the title sounds. His *History of Greek Literature,* the most voluminous and comprehensive of his works, appeared in 1890. In addition to his original writings he published translations of contemporary foreign authors, including Turgenev, and Saint Amand. Although Oliver Wendell Holmes called him "the best read man I have ever known," he refused to be ambitious, saying as he grew older that writing was more a task than a pleasure. In spite of his unusual equipment, which was encyclopedic as well as scholarly, his native temper of the student and appreciator overcame by degrees his interest in original work, and with the exception of a brief biography of his old friend, John Fiske, which appeared in 1906, he published in his later years only an occasional short article.

In 1898 he went with his family to Japan, where for three years he was professor of English at the University of Keiogijiku. After his return to Boston he remained to the end of his life an omnivorous student and reader of many languages, including Sanskrit and Russian. By nature a cosmopolite, and perhaps never quite at home in America, he lived to see himself almost the last of "Old Boston," of which he had been for years a distinguished and familiar figure. He represented the perfection of a culture that has passed, and he is remembered for an impressive and engaging personality that was itself a sort of genius. He was by nature what might be called a rationalist, if not quite a materialist, and yet was hospitable enough to say of Emerson, whose optimistic unworldliness could hardly have satisfied him, that he was "the only man I ever knew who seemed to be different from the rest of mankind." Though inclined to be exclusive in his human relations, he was altogether democratic in his appraisal of his fellow man, frowning only on what he felt to be cheap or mean or common. After a short illness he died at his home in Boston.

[C. B. Perry, *The Perrys of R.I. and Silver Creek* (1913); J. T. Morse, Jr., *Thomas Sergeant Perry, A Memoir* (1929); *Selections from the Letters of Thomas Sergeant Perry* (1929), ed. by E. A. Robinson; Boston *Transcript*, May 7, 1928.]

FOREWORD TO *THE MOUNTAIN*

Romance—in certain of its phases, at any rate—has sometimes a way of becoming so expensive and so troublesome that the slow encroachments of change will have none of it. Even romantic love—in fiction if not in fact—would appear nowadays to be looked at somewhat askance and rather as a primitive and old-fashioned waste of time and energy—while romantic hate, if possible, is faring even worse. Until recently we have looked to the Kentucky Mountains for romantic hate in its intimate and incomparable flower, yet even in that hitherto impregnable stronghold, it is seen to be yielding reluctantly a way for the inroads of education, compromise and prosaic common sense. Perhaps another age awaits us in which sense will become too common to be endured and in which we shall all find ourselves engaged in reconsidering the example of a certain illustrious Monk of Siberia as an encouragement or an escape from the paralyzing conformities and enormities of our quaintly alleged democracy, but this time is not today, nor will it be tomorrow, nor yet this year. And for that matter, perhaps the most romantic of us would hardly go so far as to wish back the feuds and furies of a rapidly vanishing tradition that must, with all its eccentricities and inconveniences, have given to life—and incidentally to death—a fillip and a jingle that may never be anticipated again with the same amount of practice and premeditation.

We of the north do not really know much about these mountain people, but we like to read about them and we like to believe that in spite of their peculiarities and their limitations they must have had rather a wonderful time. With their courage and their pride and their feuds and their moonshine, and with their incorrigible inability to understand what the United States Government, or any other government, had to do with their ideals and idiosyncrasies, they wondered, with a logic somehow still a bit annoying, what difference it made to God, who provided so obviously and impartially for either product, whether a bushel of corn should be converted ultimately into meal or into whiskey. Each of these necessary commodities was the gift of the same God that sent rain on the just and on the unjust, and each in its way was good. Unfortunately it was equally difficult for these highly individualized mountaineers to understand why a neighbor who was unpleasant or undesirable should be permitted to live; and this more serious failure on their part to perplex themselves with the spirit of a written law that not all of them could read led to many complications not unlike to that which furnishes the subject matter to Mr. Ranck's important and authentic play. Mr. Ranck was born and bred in Kentucky and he knows these people as none of us in the north could ever have known them.

While this play, *The Mountain,* is so skillfully wrought as to leave anything in the nature of a general interpretation superfluous if not absurd, there is yet one element in it, perhaps the most important of all, that may safely be emphasized for the northern reader. Most of the characters are drawn sharply for the stage and are not likely to be misinterpreted or to be left with any sort of psychic fog around them, as they speak for themselves. Yet it might be possible for a few careless readers to misinterpret the central figure, *Zeke Holston,* as merely a "bad man," with no problems of his own to ponder and to solve save those of getting what he wanted, and at any cost. But his problems are not so simple as all that, for *Zeke Holston* stands, in his own primitive and peculiar vision, as upright and as incorruptible as Oliver Cromwell or Abraham Lincoln. He simply does not understand what this new fuss and trouble is all about, or why these new-fangled notions of law and order should have come uninvited into a self-determining community where law and order had heretofore been subject pretty much to his personal interpretation; and he understands least of all why an otherwise capable and intelligent son of his should prove himself underneath his fine words and fine manners, no more and no less than a household traitor. In the father's eyes the son has gone utterly wrong, and the father would rather see the son dead than as he is. This may seem far-fetched and untrue to some of us, but it is true of this irreconcilable mountain father and has been true before of many like him.

In writing this play which has to do primarily with the father's tragic bewilderment and disillusionment, Mr. Ranck has employed a commendably artistic sincerity in giving the proper protagonist plenty of room. The love story might for sentimental or commercial reasons have been expanded more in accordance with conventional patterns, but such expansion would have contracted or distorted the picture of the father in the face of his coming catastrophe, and the play would necessarily have lost to a considerable degree the stark and cumulative distinction which it undoubtedly has. While it is first of all a play for the stage, it is one that may be read with ease and satisfaction, and with no undue demands upon the reader's visualizing imagination. This is rather rare in a play so much alive to the traditional requirements of the stage and so crowded with dynamic action. Static action, so called, has its important place in the practical drama, but its place is not in a play like *The Mountain* where it will not be found.

BRIEFS

1 I am sorry to learn that I have painted myself in such lugubrious colours. The world is not a 'prison house,' but a kind of spiritual kindergarten where millions of bewildered infants are trying to spell God with the wrong blocks.

2 After a personal experience of two summers at the MacDowell Colony at Peterborough, I can only say that I have found the place in every way fitted for the fulfilment of the purpose for which it was founded. I might write about it indefinitely, but I don't believe that I should succeed in saying more than I say now, when I tell you that my praise of the place is to be taken without any qualifications whatever. With a proper endowment, which will surely come somehow, it will be, so far as I know, the most significant thing of its kind in existence, and I am absolutely confident that there will always be a sufficient number of recognized artists — recognized professionally if not publicly — who will be glad to make use of the unprecedented opportunities that the place has to offer, during a time of which they will look back, in many cases, as one of the most fortunate and vital privileges that ever came into their lives. To one who knows the place as I do, there is something almost exasperating in the thought that its future existence should be menaced. I don't believe it can be, really, by the lack of a relatively small amount of money which would be forthcoming from many sources if its owners could be better informed as to what the late Edward MacDowell's foresight and sincerity of purpose is likely to mean, and to what extent it is likely to be felt in the future history of American literature and art.

If at any time you should wish me to say more, or something of a more detailed nature, please do not hesitate to let me know.

3 I don't know anything about the poetry of the future except that it must have, in order to be poetry, the same eternal and unchangeable quality of magic that it has always

had. Of course, it must always be colored by the age and the individual, but the thing itself will always remain unmistakable and indefinable. It seems to me a great deal of time and effort is now wasted in trying to make poetry do what it was never intended to do.

If I have a message, it ought to be pretty well revealed in the three books I've written. If it is likely to be of any great value to the race, I suppose that a part of it might be described as a faint hope of making a few of us understand our fellow creatures a little better, and to realize what a small difference there is after all between ourselves as we are and ourselves not only as we might have been but would have been if our physical and temperamental make-up and our environment had been a little different.

This may sound fatalistic, and if it does, I don't know what I can do about it. I've been called a fatalist, a pessimist and an optimist so many times that I am beginning to believe that I must be all three. I don't know what an optimist is exactly, but I have always liked the definition of one, as a man 'who doesn't care a damn what happens so long as it doesn't happen to him.'

If a reader doesn't get from my books an impression that life is very much worth living, even though it may not seem always to be profitable or desirable, I can only say that he doesn't see what I am driving at. I am glad to be able to say that several people who did not see anything in them at first, have come later to 'root' for them with considerable energy. I take this on the whole to be a good sign that I am not so silly to suppose that any amount of praise and advertising can make poetry live unless the 'magic' quality to which I referred to before is in the poetry itself. If there is such a thing as the greatest single line in English poetry, I should be inclined to say it is Wordsworth's 'The light that never was on sea or land.' I believe so firmly that poetry that is good for anything speaks for itself that I feel foolish when I try to talk about it.

4 I have nothing to say about myself. My poems speak for themselves. It is foolish to take one's self too seriously.

[*On being called a pessimist and fatalist*] When a man publishes books, he must take the consequences. A writer should not be his own interpreter. It is not the business of the writer himself to explain misunderstandings of his writings.

Universal peace has a pleasant sound, but I don't see it. I wish I did. I don't like to pose as obstructionist, but I do not agree with Alfred Noyes on this subject. The idea seems to me impracticable.

Poetry should not be propaganda, or if it is it ought to be well concealed. I suppose one might say it ought to be reprecipitated.

Good poetry must have good technique and also vision behind. Good technique is absolutely necessary. Of all the great poets the technique of Emerson comes nearest to being accidental. I agree with Noyes, by the way, that Emerson is the greatest American poet.

There is no use in talking of inspiration. The less said about inspiration and 'the frenzy' the better. I've noticed that some of the fellows who have the finest frenzies are likely to write the worst stuff.

Contemporary criticism doesn't amount to much; it takes about 50 years before we can really judge a man's work. Before that time we don't get any perspective on his place in history. Kipling will take his place among the great ones. Kipling's reputation, however, among the public has been made by his jingo pieces. The majority do not know him by his best work. The poetry of Alfred Noyes is very good. I think his best things are "The Barrel Organ" and "The Seven Singing Seamen."

I like Percy MacKaye very much. His last book, *Uriel*, is his best work, by far — that is, of his poems; I do not speak of his plays. About present day writers, if I'm going to mention any of them, William Vaughn Moody was probably the best poet of his generation. A.T. Schumann has a peculiar genius for writing ballads and rondeaus in the French form. Bliss Carman's earlier work was good, but later it has contained too many diffusions and repetitions. Other American poets whom I might mention with approval are Hermann Hagedorn, Josephine Preston Peabody (now Mrs. Marks), Louis Ledoux, Ridgely Torrence, Anna Branch and Joyce Kilmer. There are two or three others whom I can't think of now and whom I'll be sorry tomorrow I did not mention. Some of the men not known at all put out the best work.

[*Poetry today*] The English poets have a finish, a certain quality that most Americans don't have. It's a matter of tradition, I suppose. Americans have a definite advantage over the English, however, and that is their very freedom from tradition. But this has been said so much it's really not worth saying.

[*Future of poetry in America*] Things don't stay as they are. The pendulum is going all the time, though it seems to go very slowly. I have great faith in the younger men. There is every indication of better work to come. I see many poems scattered about which make me think so.

[*Post-impressionists in art*] I like to keep an open mind even for the extremist experiments in any line, though I must confess that I'm rather stumped by the cubists. There is a suggestion of charlatanism there. There are always a few extremists, and, of course, experimenting is a good thing in art as well as in science.

5 Poetry is a language that tells us, through a more or less emotional reaction, something that cannot be said. All real poetry, great or small, does this. And it seems to me that poetry has two characteristics. One is that it is, after all, undefinable. The other is that it is eventually unmistakable . . . . It is not unmistakable as soon as it is published, but sooner or later it is unmistakable.

And in the poet's lifetime there are always some people who will understand and appreciate his work. I really think that it is impossible for a real poet premanently to escape appreciation. And I can't imagine anything sillier for a man to do than to worry about poetry that has once been decently published. The rest is in the hands of Time, and Time has more than often a way of making a pretty thorough job of it. . . .

Many causes prevent poetry from being correctly appraised in its own time. Any poetry that is marked by violence, that is conspicuous in color, that is sensationally odd, makes an immediate appeal. On the other hand, poetry that is not noticeably eccentric sometimes fails for years to attract any attention.

I think that this is why so many of Kipling's worst poems are greatly overpraised, while some of his best poems are not appreciated. "Gunga Din," which is, of course, a good thing in its way, has been praised far more than it deserves, because of its oddity. And the poem beginning 'There's a whisper down the field' has never been properly appreciated. It's one of the very best of Kipling's poems, although it is marred by a few lapses of taste. One of the greatest poems, by the way, "The Children of the Zodiac," happens to be in prose.

But I am always revising my opinion of Kipling. I have changed my mind about him so often that I have no confidence in my critical judgment. That is one of the reasons why I do not like to criticise my American contemporaries.

[*Tendency to pay attention chiefly to sensational poets*] I think it applies particularly to our own time. More than ever before oddity and violence are bringing into prominence poets who have little besides these two qualities to offer the world, and some who have much more. It may seem very strange to you, but I think that a great modern instance of this tendency is the case of Robert Browning. The eccentricities of Browning's method are the things that first turned popular attention upon him, but the startling quality in Browning made more sensation in his own time than it can ever make again. I say this in spite of the fact that Browning and Wordsworth are taken as the classic examples of slow recognition. Wordsworth, you know, had no respect for the judgment of youth. It may have been sour grapes, but I am inclined to think that there was a great deal of truth in his opinion.

I think it is safe to say that all real poetry is going to give at some time or other a suggestion of finality. In real poetry you find that something has been said, and yet you find also about it a sort of nimbus of what can't be said.

This nimbus may be there — I woudn't say that it isn't there — and yet I can't find it in much of the self-conscious experimenting that is going on nowadays in the name of poetry.

I can't get over the impression that these post-impressionists in painting and most of the *vers libristes* in poetry are trying to find some sort of short cut to artistic success. I know that many of the new writers insist that it is harder to write good *vers libre* than to write good rhymed poetry. And judging from some of their results, I am inclined to agree with them.

[*Poetry written in America today better than a generation ago?*] I would hardly venture to say that. For one thing, we have no Emerson. Emerson is the greatest poet who ever wrote in America. Passages scattered here and there in his work surely are the greatest of American poetry. In fact, I think that there are lines and sentences in Emerson's poetry that are as great as anything anywhere.

Within his limits, I believe that A.E. Housman is the most authentic poet now writing in England. But, of course, his limits are very sharply drawn. I don't think that any one who knows anything about poetry will ever think of questioning the inspiration of *A Shropshire Lad.*

I think that no one will question the inspiration of some of Kipling's poems, of parts of John Masefield's *Dauber,* and some of the long lyrics of Alfred Noyes. But I do not think that either of these poets gives the impression of finality which A.E. Housman gives. But the way in which I have shifted my opinion about some of Rudyard Kipling's poems, and most of Swinburne's, makes me thing that Wordsworth was very largely right in his attitude toward the judgment of youth. But where my opinions have shifted, I think now that I always had misgivings. I fancy that youth always has misgivings in regard to what is later to be modified or repudiated.

The only effect on poetry that the war has had, so far as I know, is to produce those five sonnets by Rupert Brooke. I can't see that it has caused any poetical event. And there's no use prophesying what the war will or will not do to poetry, because no one knows anything about it. The Civil War seems to have had little effect on poetry except to produce Julia Ward Howe's "Battle Hymn of the Republic," Whitman's poems on the death of Lincoln, and Lowell's "Ode."

Should a poet be able to make a living out of poetry? Generally speaking, it is not possible for a poet to make a decent living by his work. In most cases it would be bad for his creative faculties for a poet to make as much money as a successful novelist makes. Fortunately there is no danger of that. Now, assuming that a poet has enough money to live on, the most important thing for him to have is an audience. I mean that the best poetry is likely to be written when poetry is in the air. If a poet with no obligations and responsibilities except to stay alive can't live on a thousand dollars a year (I don't undertake to say just how he is going to get it), he'd better go into some other business.

I certainly do believe that literature has lost through the poverty of poets. I don't believe in poverty. I never did. I think it is good for a poet to be bumped and knocked around when he is young, but all the difficulties that are put in his way after he gets to be 25 or 30 are certain to take something out of his work. I don't see how they can do anything else.

Some time ago you asked me how I accounted for our difficulty in making a correct estimate of the poetry of one's own time. The question is a difficult one. I don't even say that it has an answer. But the solution of the thing seems to me to be related to what I said about the quality of finality that seems to exist in all real poetry. Finality seems always to have had a way of not obtruding itself to any great extent.

6 I've never been conscious of the influence of any particular poet. One of my earliest recollections is of sitting on the floor reading "The Raven" to my father and mother; which poem, by the way, may have come as near as anything to determining my unfortunate career. The two poems that seem to have taken the strongest hold of me in those days were "The Raven" and "Lochiel's Warning," which was also inflicted without mercy upon my patient and unsuspecting parents. They never told me how much or how little they appreciated these unsolicited performances, and apparently had no suspicion of the doom that lay in wait for their eloquent offspring. There were many books of poetry in the house and I must have read nearly all of them — with the exception of Mrs. Hemans, for whom I had an ungallant and unconquerable aversion. The poets who influenced me most in those days seem to have been those who have eventually influenced me in the least. Probably Wordsworth was something of a formative influence, though I was not aware of it at the time.

I'm afraid it is useless for me to attempt to tell you what I try to do when I write a poem, for the simple reason that the thing usually does itself or isn't done at all, though I have often worked for days over a single line. Indeed, I am a terrible worker — always hammering away, but I find that the lines people read and enjoy most come of their own accord. Labor in poetry consists for the most part of making the non-spontaneous lines read as if they had written themselves. This is all right as far as it goes, but the vital part of a poem is pretty likely to come of its own accord. I doubt if any poem worth reading was ever the result of sheer skill and labor, though many a good poem has been lost through the combined ignorance and laziness of the poet.

[*What poetry should be*] I have no theory but that of naturalness. I seem to work naturally and unconsciously on the assumption that people who really care for poetry must necessarily be equipped with ears for overtones.

Don't you know what they are? I don't know how they can be defined any more than poetry can be. They might be defined as the fringe of what isn't said. I fancy that my assumption that this fringe will be discovered and recognized by the reader accounts for the fact that so many people who succeed in lighting upon what I have written were unable at first to find anything in my poems but bare words.

I am more interested in human nature than in external nature. In poetry Nature has always been more effective to me when given in glimpses.

A story hardly ever appeals to me unless some more or less universal application is in it.

I should not say there was any philosophy in my poetry beyond an instinctive protest against a materialist conception of life. When people call me a pessimist I can only wonder what they mean by pessimism.

[*Predominance of seriousness over joy in his poems*] I can only say that while I have a fairly well developed sense of humor, life has always seemed to me a pretty serious business. I haven't much to complain of in my own experience, but my observation of what others have had to endure has not encouraged me to sing the joy of living quite so loudly or so confidently as might be wished. But all this doesn't mean that I do not see more in life than a physico-chemical phenomenon. I doubt if there is such a thing in the world as a thoroughly sincere materialist. I do not know what I should do if I were one, but I am sure that I should not write poetry. In a poem called "The Burning Book" I once pictured a philosopher, but I do not pretend to be one myself.

I wrote *Merlin* because I saw a world symbol in the situation and used the Arthurian period merely as a peg to hang the picture on. There is really nothing difficult in *Merlin* if it is read as a symbol and not as a story. I wrote the poem on two themes, so to speak, which I thought were fairly obvious and not particularly original. One was that nothing can endure that is built on a false foundation, and the other is that you can't live in two worlds at the same time. King Arthur knew that he had built on a false foundation and realized pretty well what was coming. Merlin knew what was coming when he surrendered himself to Vivian. He could see as Arthur couldn't what was to spring up out of the ruins. In *Lancelot,* to be published soon, the symbolism is not so much in evidence and the poem may be read simply as a story if the reader prefers it that way. I must admit that that is rather more than may be said of *Merlin.*

[*The "new spirit" in poetry*] I think it is the result of a gradual tendency to break away from old poetic diction. In a way it is more subtle and less obvious. When I published my first book more than twenty-five years ago I was accused of breaking away from accepted standards too much. I had no public when I began. My public has been accumulated, more or less under protest, very slowly.

What I did seemed perfectly natural to me. I had no idea of establishing any new movement in poetry. As I look back I see that I wrote as I did without considering how much of the old poetical machinery I left behind. I see now that I have always disliked inversions as well as many other conventional solemnities which seem to have had their day. I could never, even as a child, see any good reason why the language of verse should be distorted almost out of recognition in order to be poetical.

I have only one objection to free verse and that is that it seems to me to be a makeshift.

About the best I can say is that the best free verse that I have seen contains subject matter for good poems. But in saying this I wish it clearly understood that I am stating merely my personal opinion. I have no quarrel with the writers of free verse and I can at least be broadminded enough to hope that I am wrong in my notion that most of them are wasting their time and energy. If free verse is as easy to write as it is difficult to read, one can hardly be surprised that we have so much of it. My attitude, however, may be prejudiced and entirely wrong. Only a few years ago, as I said, I was criticized as a radical, but I may be a conservative, after all.

7 My "philosophy" — so far as I have one — seems to me fairly obvious, in that it consists mainly in the assumption that if life is not something more than a material phenomenon it had much better never have been, and that such an interpretation is impossible — for me, at least — in the light of inferences, intuition, and reason; wherefore I must be, in the last analysis, an "optimist."

8 I may as well be honest at the outset and tell you that your question as to why American colleges do not produce more poets and novelists is one that I cannot answer. Barrett Wendell once asked me if I had taken the regular course in English composition at Harvard, and when I told him that I had taken only one year of it, he said, "You're damned lucky." This was more than twenty years ago: and since then, so far as one can see, no overpowering literary geniuses have emerged from Harvard, or from anywhere else. I'm afraid the only answer is that they don't happen very often — though let us hope that a few may be growing somewhere on earth. I believe in colleges, but I doubt if they have much to do with the genesis of literature, except in indirect ways.

9 Please let me write a few words as one who is greatly interested in the Poetry Society of South Carolina, and as

one who believes that its existence is significant not only to the South, but to the North and the East and the West. Many poems that have been written by contemporary Southern authors are of a quality to make us up here in the North wish that a few Palmettoes might be persuaded to sprout and spread themselves along with our native pines and hemlocks which are [not] always murmuring.

10 [*"Tact"*] Good Lord! if people find that obscure, I wonder what they make of some of my other things . . . . I like to leave a poem with a fringe round it.

11 Twenty-five years ago I was a radical.

12 I hardly know what to say about "The Whip," except that it is supposed to be a literal and not a figurative instrument. In this poem — not to mention a few others — I may have gone a little too far and given the reader too much to carry. If he refuses to carry it, perhaps I have only myself to blame. I am inclined to believe that this particular poem is not altogether satisfactory or very important.

13 As far as I can make out, poetry is a sort of secretion. It is either there or it isn't, and I doubt very much if the poet himself has very much to say about it. At any rate, it has been proved that no amount of labor and striving will produce it.

There is a lot of brilliance and dash among the younger writers, but it would be a good thing for them all if they would go back and read Shakespeare and the Old Testament for a few years. Young poets make a mistake to publish their work when they are too young. They get a pin-feather fame as boys, which is detrimental to their later development. Of course, there isn't very much poetry in the world . . . .

There are never more than four or five poets in the world at the same time, and no one knows who they are until they have been dead half a century.

When William Vaughn Moody and I began to write there were about seven or eight poets whom one heard of in this country. In those days it was almost impossible to get a book of poems published. Now it is almost impossible not to get them published.

There is some mysteriousness about that inability to judge contemporary poetry, but it has always been so. I think, on the whole, that American poetry, at present, is more vital and significant than most that is being written in England. But one of the great faults with American poetry is that it is altogether too much a reaching out for short cuts to glory. Many of the younger writers seem to have lost all standards, or, rather, they give the impression that they never had any. They show no end of cleverness, but they don't know really how to work.

Most people seem to forget that poetry is the most exhausting and tyrannical of professions and they turn it into a sort of mild dissipation. I can't speak for others, but I don't see how a man can write poetry and do anything else. Probably the public will never understand that however much inspiration there may be poetry is the hardest kind of work.

14 While I am very glad to know that you are to review my book, I must beg to evade your request for my personal opinion as to what poem in it is best. Possibly I am the last person to know.

15 In sending this brief message to Percy MacKaye for his fiftieth birthday I have the double pleasure of greeting a good friend and an altogether remarkable man. MacKaye seems to be one of the very few living writers who will leave behind him at least one unquestionable work of genius, if not more than one. Genius is a dangerous word and often too loosely employed, but *The Scarecrow* will endure.

16 My theory of art is very simple and is not new. The great bulk of art of all kinds consists merely in giving out of what has been absorbed from others. The best, however, is a miracle of sheer genius, producing what the world has never before had.

Good romance is highly creative and important. Dickens is so immense that he still has the power of giving one strong reactions, even though the present literary trend is so much against him. Hugo I have not read since I was a boy, and I do not remember him sufficiently well to give an opinion in his case. I doubt that *The Prisoner of Zenda* would enjoy its former popularity, however, if it were published to-day. Only romances of the greatest caliber could stem the present tide [of literary realism].

17 [*Robinson Jeffers*] You have an amazing fertility and daring.

18 In point of fact, I recommend a careful reading of my books to anyone who wishes to become an incurable optimist.

[*Avon's Harvest*] You know, ghosts don't leave knives. All the reviewers so far have made that mistake. It is simply a more excruciating form of mental torture which he contrived when he let Avon think he was a ghost.

19 [*Has no literary influences*] I look upon poetry as a treasure to draw from.

I have no theories about poetry. I believe a man writes the kind of poetry he writes and that's all there is to it.

Except in the case of the incurable poet, the vein is likely to run out with youth. Because the [*at this point the previous line is repeated and the line that should follow is omitted*] tistic dissipations but, as a rule, it doesn't mean anything. I always tell young people not to publish anything until they're thirty. If they'd wait they'd save themselves a lot of needless heartache. I try to dissuade them from publishing at all, but that's impossible. The mere fact that they do stop and do other things shows that the poetic impulse isn't strong enough to cause them to make any great sacrifice for it. An artist in any line who isn't willing to sacrifice everything within reason should find a new occupation as soon as possible.

Sooner or later the real poems are likely to be found. I suppose there are great poems buried. But I don't believe there are very many. On the other hand, I don't believe that any poet whose work bulks can be definitely placed until he has been dead half a century.

[*Does Ernest Newman's theory about Beethoven's "unconscious" genius in music apply to poets?*] The theory applies pretty well. I don't think the artist has much to say about his own artistic capital. But I don't think Beethoven was entirely unconscious of what he was doing all the time. The only intelligent way to consider the artist is as an instrument played upon by something he does not understand. But there's a providential gift of self-esteem which usually makes him think he's doing it himself. And that applies particularly to the bad artist.

This is a mechanical, material age. But it is also a great intellectual age. I think there's a great deal of conscious groping for an ideal, something that isn't food or lodging. Great rewards are set aside for material accomplishments. Maybe they always were. The glamour of the past blinds us to actual conditions. Take Rembrandt. We read of a Rembrandt painting having been sold for a quarter of a million and forget that ten years after his death it might have been bought for $10, and that he died almost in obscurity. As we look back upon the Elizabethan and Victorian ages, they seem poetical to us, but I doubt if they were poetical to the Elizabethans and the Victorians.

About one in 1,000 reads poetry with a fair degree of intelligence.

[*Longfellow and Tennyson*] It is rather the fashion to put them into the discard, but that won't do. Longfellow was always an artist and people mustn't forget that.

When I was younger I used to read all the time. I have come to the age when novels look wrong. Unless it's a detective story it's pretty hard for me to read a book 300 or 400 pages long . . . .When I want to read poetry I usually read a play of Shakespeare over again . . . . The dramatic element in poetry always appealed to me. As far back as I can remember the speeches and scenes in Shakespeare always gave me the biggest thrill.

20 [*First collection of poems*] I arranged them in manuscript form, gave them the title *The Torrent and The Night Before,* after the first and last poems, and sent them to a publisher.

I knew that it was then difficult to get poetry published in America, but I thought that a publisher would be glad to get them. They came back. I was surprised, and hurt a little, I suppose. I sent them out again. Again I was surprised, but hurt this time. As the manuscript acquired the chronic habit of coming back, I got over being surprised, and got mad. I felt that all that work shouldn't go for nothing. At all events,

I wanted to find out who was right, the publishers or I. So I arranged for publication at my own expense through the Riverside Press of Boston.

[*Dedication of The Torrent and The Night Before*] I wouldn't mind if you could forget that dedication. It was a cocky thing to do. I must have been conceited and still a bit mad. Maybe it attracted some attention. Anyhow, the edges on some of them were cut in the course of time.

[*Titus Munson Coan*] A trifling incident occurred while I was getting rid of those blue books which had interesting results — for me at least. In Gardiner we had a group of young men who had formed a kind of club. I don't know that we called it a club. Anyhow, we had a meeting place. It was a room over a store on the main street. We went there to talk and smoke. We talked about literary things, and one of the boys played the fiddle.

One summer night toward the close of the summer of 1896, our gathering broke up and we trooped down-stairs to find that it was pouring rain. One of my friends said he was going back to hunt his umbrella. I went with him. While he was looking for it, I picked up and read by the light of the gas a little magazine which lay on the table. In it was a quatrain that struck me as pretty good. It was by a Doctor Coan, and his address was given. I didn't know it at the time, but later I learned that he was an editor of a sort, assisting amateur literary aspirants to prepare their compositions for publication.

Forthwith, I sent Doctor Coan a copy of *The Torrent and The Night Before*. Back came a letter of the most enthusiastic commendation, one of the most enthusiastic that the blue book got at the time. Among other things, he said that if I ever got down to New York he wanted to get in touch with me.

[*Alfred H. Louis*] Old Mr. Louis! I should never have known him and "Captain Craig" would never have been written except for the accident of my friend's forgetting his umbrella on a rainy night in '96.

Old shabby bearded, and poor — God knows how poor he was! — God knows how he kept body and soul together! — he looked like a prophet out of the Old Testament. An Englishman, an intellectual Jew, a graduate of Trinity College, and a convert to the Catholic faith, he was versed in the religions and philosophies of all the world, and the most learned man I have ever encountered.

Some way or other he managed to live. Somebody gave him enough to keep him alive. Doctor Coan helped him out, and there were others. One way or another the ravens looked after old Mr. Louis.

I came to know him well, and to feel that I wanted to perpetuate his personality, that air of greatness which there was about him and which was like a legend, with no date in Circumstance, or Time, or Thing. He is the central figure of "Captain Craig." He *is* Craig. Of course he wasn't a captain of anything. He didn't belong to the Navy, never had sea-faring experience. He was a Captain of Souls so to speak, a General of Philosophy, a derelict adrift . . . .

Old Mr. Louis knew of the use to which I put him. He read the manuscript. He laughed and was immensely pleased. He was tickled, as I have no doubt his ghost will be to-day by this association of him with the original of Captain Craig. The other characters of the poem, who also were taken somewhat from the life, never saw him. It just pleased me to place him in that environment. And if anyone, reading "Craig" to-day, should feel that the Tilbury boys, while feeding the Captain crusts and keeping life in his half-starved body, throve prodigiously on his philosophic outpourings, thus receiving far more than they gave, I should be glad. It is a thought I meant to put there.

[*Theodore Roosevelt offers a job*] The thing that astonished me was that the President of the United States should be able to find the time to dig up a young poet out of the rather dark obscurity that veiled him from view and to think of ways to help. It wasn't so astonishing that he should be *disposed* to help. He was that kind of a man. There were depths in his nature which, during his lifetime, he was not too often credited with.

After I had informed the President that I should be glad of a chance to do anything at which I could make a living, there was some talk, I believe, of making me an immigration inspector with a location in some foreign country. However, I preferred American soil, and New York to any other place. Presently I was informed of an opening in the Special Agent's Office of the Customs House.

[*MacDowell Colony*] It is to the Colony that I owe the opportunity I had always wanted, and never expected to get — the chance for sustained, uninterrupted work. I am certain that many of my books never would have materialized except for what we have come to call "the Peterborough idea."

[*Long obscurity as a poet*] There were times when it seemed that the day would never break. But remember one thing: When a man has something that he very much wants to do, something that matters a great deal to him, whether or not it does to anybody else, he isn't likely to think so very much about the outcome. If a thing of that kind once gets hold of you it isn't hard to work without recognition or encouragement. I was always fortunate in being able to do my work in my own way, with the confidence that the end would take care of itself.

[*What it takes, more than just faith, to make a poet*] The secret of it all, it seems to me, lies in this: Behind any achievement worth calling by the name, you will find a man who, in some way or other, early or late, has hit upon what he can do. People should *find out what they can do* — which is something that many people never discover at all.

But watch any man who is swimming along, making a go of his enterprise. The chances are that he likes it. Presumably, it *goes* because he likes it. Take George M. Cohan, who is undoubtedly a genius in his field. He likes what he is doing; he does it well; he communicates that liking to all of us.

[*When he determined to become a poet*] Whenever it was that I began really to write. After that I never doubted it would come out all right, if I kept at it.

I felt as certain that this was what I should *try* to do as any boy who has been expecting from his earliest memory to follow his father's footsteps into the law. My conviction was that my contribution, if any, was to be in artistic form. It was just a Fact, with a capital F perhaps. I wasn't particularly elated by the prospect. I had read enough to know that writing poetry didn't mean a bed of roses. Rather, I felt that I was 'in for it.' But I wasn't frightened. It seemed like a gigantic venture. I anticipated hardships. Looking back, I'm surprised that they weren't much greater than they proved to be.

I don't believe that a man can do with great success anything that is much above or below his natural abilities. However, if a man has the innate ability to do a specific thing, there is a fair chance that he will *will* to do it, and *try hard*. *Vice versa,* if he wants to do it so much that he will try hard, that may almost be taken as a sure sign that he has the *ability* to do it.

Heredity has a good deal to do with it — perhaps everything, when it comes to the arts. In the great shuffle of transmitted characteristics, traits, abilities, and aptitudes, the man who fixes on something definite in life that he must do, at the expense of anything else, if necessary, has presumably got something that, for him, should be recognized as the Inner Fire. For *him,* that is the Gleam, the Vision and the Word! He'd better follow it. The greatest adventure he'll ever have on this side is following where it leads.

21 [*To would-be poets*] If you've got yourself into that trap there's nothing I or anyone else can say to get you out.

[*Poetry as a living*] Well, if you keep at it for forty years you may have about half as much as a good carpenter . . . . You've got to get money from some other source, whether you steal it or inherit it . . . . Then there's getting married . . . . I suppose it would be better if you taught something other than literature . . . . Don't go into journalism! It hurts a man's style every time. Even Kipling. His things have been marred by journalism.

Nine-tenths of poetry is *how* it's done.

Don't look for me in my poetry, because you won't find me . . . . Of course, the mood — the thought, but you won't find me . . . In that one ["On the Night of a Friend's Wedding"], to be sure, there's a little, but not much.

[*Merlin* and *Lancelot*] World War poems. If you read them with that in mind you'll get more out of them. The passing of an old order and the beginning of a new. I didn't intend to write *Tristram,* but somehow it couldn't be denied.

[*Tristram*] I read Swinburne to avoid collisions. Swinburne follows the French version and I rather hit off both French and English. I go back, more, to Malory.

[*"The Man Against the Sky"*] The whole ending of the poem is ironical, even sarcastic. Of course, the implication is that there *is* an existence [after death].

[*Philosophy of failure in his poems*] I've always rather liked the queer, odd sticks of men, that's all. The fat, sleek, successful alderman isn't interesting. He isn't interesting.

[*Laramie Cavender*] She is a projection of Cavender's brain. Such things do happen, you know. Though I don't suppose one ever happened that was as long as that. But that's artistic license.

Don't publish a book till you're thirty. Thirty's time enough.

Matthias is better than *Roman Bartholow.* But not better than parts of *Bartholow.* Parts of that are as good as anything I've done.

The only model I ever used was an old English Jew for Captain Craig. I just transferred him to my mythical town [Tilbury], which is more or less Gardiner. Of course, people are always thinking I use models.

[*Amy Lowell*] She was really quite medieval. She should have lived in Renaissance Italy. She'd have enjoyed poisoning people. A grand talker. But always slaying six or eight people an evening. [Joseph Auslander's essay on Amy is] a very good portrait, though I don't know if it's always in good taste. —But then, neither was Amy. O yes, she had a personality all right. But I'm afraid when her work is sifted there's not much there.

[*Edgar Lee Masters*] bitter — he's bitter as gall.

[*Carl Sandburg*] I don't care so much for his poetry. But then, we can't help those things.

[*Robert Frost*] He's a good fellow . . . . Going back to those *North of Boston* poems, I find they don't wear so well. Well, Frost is a kind of professional farmer. He is a bit self-conscious, but harmlessly so. He's a good fellow — a good fellow.

You know, I understand they teach Frost and me in the schools now. I don't know which one they teach first.

[*Whittier might be a*] sounder poet than Longfellow. Longfellow was more of an artist than Whittier. If it weren't for those sonnets we'd be very different poets.

[*Emerson*] He had the real juice.

[*Poe achieved a music no one else ever had*], without jingle, too. But I never have read a poem of his in which something didn't strike me wrong.

[*Wondered if Walt Whitman were*] as great as some people think he is. [Parts of *Leaves of Grass* were all right and] some of the shorter things he wrote as an old man were good . . . . [Robinson's "sonnet" on Whitman] It wasn't a sonnet; it was a piece of blank verse. I was very young when I wrote it, but I knew all the time I was writing it that I didn't really mean it.

[*T.S. Eliot*] Certainly the best of the younger men, but of course most of his best lines were written by other people.

[*E.E. Cummings*] If I were younger maybe I'd like that sort of thing. Well, they [the younger poets] think I'm an old fogey, and I guess I am an old fogey.

[*George Crabbe*] I have a set of Crabbe. Somebody thought I was crazy about him because I wrote a sonnet about him, and gave me a set . . . . There are good things in him.

[I] would have done the dramatic monologues whether or not there had been a Browning.

22 [*William Gillette*] As one who has known and admired you, from the audience, for about half a century, please let me add my thanks and congratulations to the many that you will be receiving at this time.

Incidentally, let me thank you also for your *Astounding Crime*. I hope you will see your way to commit another that will be equally astounding and satisfactory.

23 As I grow older I find myself less inclined, if possible, to indulge in the luxuries of publicity. I am still human, however, and am glad to know that there are several people somewhere who like what I have done, or some of it.

24 The way of the transgressor is said to be hard, but it is [no] harder than that of the poet or the musical composer or

the man who invents a new machine. The writing of poetry is as essentially a profession as is engineering or law, and if I am a poet, it is only because poetry has dominated my life ever since I was old enough to understand the fundamentals of music and verse.

The real poet, like the real artist, is a freak of nature, and for this reason no sane man would attempt to prophesy the future developments in this field of letters.

If the future of English poetry is unpredictable in its specific aspects, there are certain broad lines of development along which it must necessarily proceed. The present tendency of poetry appears to be away from sordid realism toward what may be described as romantic realism, although the stilted poetic diction of the nineteenth century romantic school may never again be achieved, or is there any reason why it could be. I am essentially a classicist in poetic composition, and I believe that the accepted media for the masters of the past will continue to be used in the future. There is, of course, room for infinite variety, manipulation and invention within the limits of traditional forms and meters, but any violent deviation from the classic mean may be a confession of inability to do the real thing, poetically speaking.

I am not sure that there has been any really great name, with the possible exception of Swinburne, added to the list of English poets since Tennyson. It is difficult to estimate the relative positions of Masefield, Kipling and Hardy, because they are essentially writers of the present time. If a man is important enough to arouse controversy, a contemporary estimate of his worth must of necessity be unreliable. It is a problem for the years to solve. There are many minor poets as influential and significant in their way as the greater masters of verse. The name of A.E. Housman, for instance, is as secure to fame as that of any poet of the last seventy-five years. He is a king in a small kingdom, despite the fact that he published his *Shropshire Lad* at a time when the name of Rudyard Kipling filled almost the whole poetic horizon.

I am frequently asked why the war has not produced more great English poetry. It is my opinion that modern war is not a poetic subject. There have been the cries of a few individual singers, but in general war destroys more than it produces, and its reputed romance is fast being discredited.

No poet can be an adequate judge of his own writing, and only the passage of time can set the seal of authentic genius on anything written today. Whatever laurels I may receive must, to be good for anything, be green long after I and my generation have withered. Poetic experience can penetrate far beyond human expression, but I do not pretend to be a philosopher and I do not like to be called one.

25 While the matter is certainly settled for you, as a good Catholic, there is room for an infinite amount of groping and searching for many who cannot accept the tenets of your Church, or of any other. It is evident that science is not giving, at any rate, any satisfactory substitute for religion, which is perhaps becoming more and more a thing for each one to feel for himself. I should say too you might find many evidences of this in recent verse.

Outside the Catholic Church, religion is having a pretty hard time nowadays.

26 "Partnership" was published originally under the title, "The Wife of Palissy" . . . In a misguided moment I changed it — with some notion, I suppose, of giving the poem a more general application. "It" is (or was) obviously one of Palissy's porcelains. Now it can be almost anything.

27 I am more of a transcendentalist than many of my friends are willing to believe. When I write, I am only the agent of

something-or-other. The real poet, like the real artist, is a freak of nature.

[*With Conrad Aiken on a night train from Liverpool to London*] There was no restaurant car on the train and neither of us had had a thing to eat or drink since luncheon. All the sleeping compartments were full, and it looked like a long, cold, weary trip, when suddenly I remembered two imperial quarts of Burke's Irish whiskey in my grip. It was astonishing how soon we were at Euston, and just as we drew into the train shed we finished the last drop in the second bottle. I felt fine and was out being entertained in Romano's by noon, but Aiken, pooh, he was no drinker at all. It was a week before he got out of the Charing Cross Turkish Baths.

28 Yes, the failures are so much more interesting. Then, too, there is more drama in the lives of failures than in the smug, complacent stories of material success.

I don't know whether I am a great poet or not. Time alone can tell about that. But I do know that I have never consciously injured any one. And that at least is something.

29 [*His favorites among his works*] I have never given the matter much thought. My favorites are, perhaps, "Ben Jonson," *The Man Who Died Twice, Merlin, Lancelot, Tristram, Cavender's House.*

30 [*Captain Craig*] I suppose the book contains some of my best and some of my worst work.

[*Gardiner, Maine*] may be responsible, in a shadowy way, for Tilbury Town.

31 In after years nothing tastes the same as in our youth.

32 [*Matthias at the Door*] I am tempted to make an unusual request, or suggestion, which you may act upon or not. There is a general tendency to mispronounce Matthias, and I wonder if in parentheses under the title in the first advertisements, and in a short paragraph of publisher's news, you could say (pronounced Matthi-as). An accent on the first syllable completely destroys the metre of many of the lines. I don't know just what — if anything — can be done about it.

33 . . . my "philosophy" . . . is mostly a statement of my inability to accept a mechanistic interpretation of the universe and of life. As I see it, my poetry is not pessimistic, nothing of an infinite nature can be proven or disproven in finite terms — meaning words — and the rest is probably a matter of one's individual ways of seeing and feeling things. There is no sense in saying that this world is not a pretty difficult place, but that isn't pessimism. The real pessimist sees too much of one thing, and the optimist is too likely to see what he wishes to see — or perhaps not to see at all beyond the end of his famous nose. I still wish that you were writing about my poetry — of which my philosophy is only a small part, and probably the least important . . . .

34 When a man's work is of sufficient importance to arouse controversy, contemporary criticism can only search in a fog of conjecture for the place that time will ultimately find for it. But I am one of those who believe that the best of Vachel Lindsay's work will live for a long time; for there is nothing else like it, and the best of it has spontaneity and a mark of the inevitable that comes only by what we have to call genius. He will be easy to remember, and as difficult to forget.

35 1. My interest in poetry goes back almost as far as I can remember.

2. There were not only days, but several years, when patience (with and without work) and faith were my main supports.

3. Perhaps "The Man Against the Sky" comes as near as anything to representing my poetic vision — as you are good enough to call it.

4. I cannot attempt to say what will happen to poetry in America during the next two or three decades. A new light is likely to shine at any time.

36 — be sure that you know what you want to do. If you are sure of that, success will probably take care of itself — so long as you do not want to write poetry.

37 I tried many experiments—ballads, quatrains, villanelles. I tried many forms, but I was not really interested in them except as exercises.

[*Always knew he would write poetry*?] Yes, I think so, but I knew from the beginning that I was in for it. I did enough to bring down trouble on my head, but I have been treated well — I have had much less difficulty than I *might* have had. I had my experience early, but it went *deep*.

[*Poetic diction*] Even with his early poems Robinson was "interested in using an idiom unfamiliar as poetry." He said that it took him twenty years to accustom people to his method. This poetic diction was to preserve the rhythms of ordinary speech within the traditional forms; . . . his best poetry is "somewhere" in the Arthurian poems because, he explained, "The romantic framework enabled me to use my idiom more freely."

Poetry must be music, not that it must jingle, but it *must be music*. And that is the defect of free verse. Maybe it's possible to write musical free verse, but I've never read any. And it's not memorable either. I cannot recall a single poem written in free verse, can you?

[*Second to being music*] poetry must bite.

There is no such thing as the sonnet, there are only individual sonnets.

[*Sitting in a movie theatre*] Suddenly I saw Flammonde and I could hear the poem quite clearly. All the lines were there and I only had to write them down.

I like to be familiar with my characters and their development before I start a poem. *Tristram* took two entire summers to write and I worked out its structure somewhat as a playwright would work out a play.

[*Arthurian trilogy as allegory*] (They tell of) the breaking-up of the old order. It is all there — it is all quite clear.

But I am not a playwright. A play must be *direct* — there is no chance for a movement of light and shade.

[*His male characters*] Well, for that matter, I suppose anyone who leaves the middle of the road is abnormal in one way or another.

[It is] more interesting to write about failure than success . . . . Hamlet was a failure.

[*Fate and folly*] I think a man's pattern is there before him, but it's difficult to discuss these ideas, we're getting metaphysical and our terminology may mean such different things . . . . I think man is more than he seems.

Ideas are, of course, inseparable from the medium, but much memorable poetry is not important for what is said.

Somehow I feel that Whitman seems greater than he is. Anyway, I feel that whatever power he had was as a poet — not a thinker.

But if you want to find out about my 'Transcendentalism' read *The Man Against the Sky* and *Matthias at the Door* — it's in those poems.

It is impossible to believe that it is all for nothing — such waste would be inconceivable.

38 You might say in your preface that *Merlin, Lancelot* and *Tristram* — taken together as a sort of unit — appear to me as likely to last as anything that I have written, but I cannot say which of the short poems are better than are the others — though I could easily name some that are not.

39 [*My public is*] cut in two: some like them [poems] long, others like them short. And it is hard to please them both.

[On being called a pessimist] There is no sense in the charge at all. There is no sense, though, in pretending that life is all a rose garden; no sense, that is, if one uses his eyes. I suppose that the charge of my being a pessimist comes from a deterministic, a fatalistic note in my work. I suppose I do believe that we are pretty much what we are.

It annoys me to hear talk about my philosophy of life. I am not a philosopher. I don't intend to be one. But I have been criticized for writing so much about 'failures.' Well, isn't it the people who fail who are more interesting than the others? They are — at least for the purpose of dramatic poetry. There is nothing poetic, and usually nothing dramatic about anyone who is a 'success.'

In *Talifer* I deliberately set out to be light, and to write a comedy. Most people who have read the book get what I was driving at but some of the critics fumble at it, and resent my being cheerful. I don't know why. It is not unusual, ever for me. For in all my dramatic poems there is an undercurrent of comedy and humor. I do not see why people should be surprised to see more of it. But then, that's all right. I'm too old to bother about such things.

I am a little tired about hearing of "Richard Cory." I suppose it is because it is concise and clear and has a sharp conclusion that people like to remember it.

Whenever I talk of my own work, I wish I hadn't. I have not much to say.

I think we must leave my contemporaries out of it. I don't mind your saying, though, that I think a lot of Robert Frost's work.

No one wants to write what's already written. We don't want the Victorian style repeated. But this modern stuff, without punctuation or capitals, I don't see how they can expect to go far with it. But they look upon me as an old timer. They may be right.

I think there is a main road in all the arts. These young fellows, I think, are off the road. But that doesn't mean that everything which rolls over it must be like what went before.

No one who writes poetry can tell why he wrote it. I write these long poems of mine because they come to me and have to be written. I have a wonderful time when writing.

Generally speaking, American historical subjects are too close. There is, however, a lot of dramatic poetry in the Revolutionary period. I don't see why our poets are not ready for that.

Sociology — whatever the word means — usually kills poetry, art of any kind. All propaganda that is permissible in art has got to be pretty thoroughly disguised.

So far as I can make out, poetry is like a vein of ore in the earth. You can't dig out more than is there. Some have a thin vein of fine gold, others a thicker vein that is not so pure, and I don't believe much can be done about it. A.E. Housman — his work, don't you agree, is pretty nearly perfect. But I don't think there is any more there. There is not much real poetry in the world anyway. If anyone can dig up a little, he's lucky.

If I care enough about a poem to write it, it gives me pleasure. "John Evereldown" and "Luke Havergal" [are] 'young poems' written when [I] was twenty-three. I don't know where they came from. They just came, out of the air.

40 There seems to me to be no question as to the enduring quality of A.E. Housman's poetry. I do not think of any living writer whose work is likely to live longer, if as long. For some reason I find it difficult to select the two or three of his poems that I like best, and that may be the highest compliment I could pay to his work.

41 I am a fatalist as far as poetry is concerned. If a man has poetry in him, it will out; if not, he will produce only verse. There is too much verse and too little poetry in the world today.

42 [Alfred] Noyes is a man I like. He is a happy man — that is in so far as a poet can be really happy except when he is actually producing poetry.

[*Arnold Bennett*] His greatness does weigh heavily upon him — but he manages to support it.

43 Why must people talk? I have never been able to understand why people must talk. And they talk for hours. I hear about one-tenth of what is said. Ah, I don't know what to think about people.

[*Climbing Mt. Monadnock*] I would rather hear you tell me of it. You can't work if you use up your energy. That is not the way I conduct life . . . . If I go somewhere and have a good time it is all right. The danger is I go and do not have a good time. Then I lose energy.

I was born to suffer. Even as a child I thought the quotation should end at the words: *Suffer little children.* I have never grasped the rest of the meaning.

I am very gregarious really. Though no one seems to believe it.

44 [*Boris Todrin*] I have been reading your poems with a deal of interest, and at times with a great deal of surprise; much of your work is remarkable. You appear to have an unusual gift.

I should not be so frank if I were not entirely sincere, and should not go to the trouble of writing all this if I were not really impressed by the quality and the promise that is revealed in this early work of yours.

I am sure you will understand by this that I am sincerely interested in your work and that I look for something altogether out of the ordinary from you. In fact you have given me that already.

45 [*"Mr. Flood's Party"*] I am sending you the poem that caused all that commotion in the office of *Collier's*. I am still at a loss to detect its difficulties or its dangers, or to believe that the public is made up entirely of imbeciles.

[*Avon's Harvest*] I supposed, by the way, that the knife would be enough to show that the other fellow was not drowned, but chose merely to let Avon think so. Maybe I had better add a few lines to the collected edition to make this entirely clear.

Kipling's poetry is better than most people think.

They praise me for never doing anything but writing poetry. I would always have taken a job if I had known how to get one and keep it.

46 I wish I were a good talker — like Frost, for instance. But I am not, and I never expect to be. So I can only try to put the best of myself into my writing, and let it go at that.

[*Thomas Hardy as poet*] He stumbles along a good deal, but somehow he usually manages to get there.

[*Walt Whitman*] I may be wrong; I probably am. But I have never been able to find so much in him.

Emerson wrote some of the purest poetry we have in America — though not a great deal of it. The trouble is, nobody reads it. And most people don't know it exists. They get sidetracked to "Self-Reliance" or "The Oversoul."

[*Elinor Wylie*] You know how it was with Elinor: if you wanted to get along best with her, it was well to bow down a little. And since I never found it very easy to do that to any one, I suppose we never saw quite so much of each other as we might have. But she was a poet just the same. I can't say that I cared so much for some of her first work. It impressed me as being brittle. But somewhere along the way toward the end she struck fire.

Don't pay a damned bit of attention to what anybody says. If you begin to listen to what people say, you are done for. Just now they are all busy telling me that I ought not to be writing those long poems. Maybe not. But how can anybody know — anybody except myself? They happen to be the thing that's in my blood; so I've got to write them. No, sir-r! Mostly we go alone. And if a man hasn't learned that, he hasn't learned anything.

[*Oscar Wilde*] That poor devil interests me, and I like *Dorian Gray*.

[*Reviewers*] How they find me a pessimist, and all that, just because I can't subscribe to their ready-made little notions of things, particularly the future, is beyond me. As a matter of fact, I am more of an optimist than any of them — if they must have it in their own words — for when I look at this life without the rosy spectacles and try to see it as a thing in itself, as the final word, it is too absurd to be thought of. You've got to add something, just to make sense.

Those years at Harvard were no more painful than some of the others . . . . I wonder more and more just where I might have come out if I had never seen Harvard Square as I did. Of course, I might have come out farther ahead than I've ever got. But one thing is certain: there was something in the place that changed my way of looking at a good many things.

[*The Torrent and The Night Before*] I wanted a hearing and that seemed to be about the only way to get it. I can't say that the volume exactly set the world on fire.

[*Reviewers*] If only they had said something about me! It would not have mattered what. They could have called me stupid or crazy if they liked. But they said nothing. Nobody devoted as much as an inch to me. I did not exist.

[*His daily output*] My smallest was when I once spent a month on a couple of lines; and my largest was once when I was going strong on the latter part of *Tristram*. I put down a hundred and ten lines on that day. But I was good for nothing for the rest of the week. Still I didn't mind. I never came up to that in anything else, though, that I recall, unless maybe in *Lancelot,* though I have often enough put down fifty or sixty, and once in a while seventy. It was more likely to be the ten without the hundred — twenty, or thirty. Of course, after you get going in a long poem, it comes faster than in a sonnet or a lyric . . . . my idea is to put the first draft down as fast as I can, and then rewrite as slow as I can.

. . . the ghost of Cavender's dead wife was a projection of Cavender's own mind . . . . What I tried to do, of course, was to create an extension or projection of Cavender's own mind that could stand off and examine him without mercy — and without ordinary hate.

47 [*Custom House job*] It is the third offer that has come my way through Roosevelt's influence. I had a note from him regarding this one that was short and to the point: "Good salary. Little work. Soft snap!"

[*Harvard training*] Had I continued to listen to that sort of stuff I would have lost every particle of creative instinct I possess! I don't know why it affected me in that manner, but it *did!*

[*Richard Burton*] Certainly he is one of America's most worthwhile poets and an inspiration to me and other 'authors of metrical composition,' — as the dictionary defines us.

48 [*Had his sense of humor lengthened his life?*] I think my life has lengthened my sense of humor.

49 [Carlyle's *Sartor Resartus*] a great poem.

[Whitman's "When Lilacs Last in the Dooryard Bloom'd"] If that's not poetry, it is something greater than poetry.

If I could have done anything else on God's green earth, I never would have written poetry. There was nothing else I could do, and I had to justify my existence.

I can't do anything but write poetry and perhaps I can't do even that, but I'm going to try. I don't expect recognition while I live but if I thought I could write something that would go on living after I'm gone, I'd be satisfied with an attic and a crust all my life.

Somehow I can't consider myself in the same universe with a person who doesn't love Dickens . . . . The first two hundred pages of *Dombey and Son* are the best thing Dickens ever did.

I was born with my skin inside out.

This stuff of mine is never going to be heard from in my lifetime. But, fifty or sixty years after I am dead, someone may find something in it.

I simply don't get anything from pictures [paintings] and I can't understand how anyone else does.

This hypothesis is the only satisfactory explanation of life. We are living in hell, and some of us do know it.

There are not enough people who would know what I am saying, even if they did read me. A poet's trade is a martyr's trade.

Make clear to those people who say I gave up great things to write poetry, that there was only one thing in the world that I could give up, and that was writing poetry, for that was all that meant anything to me.

[*King Jasper*] Zoë isn't intended to symbolize Life. Zoë is knowledge, and the child of King Jasper, who is ignorance. Without ignorance, there can be no knowledge.

50 The great art of life is to suffer without worrying.

51 [*Why he lived "with nothing but a bed"*] Because I am a faithful servant of Apollo.

[*Why he did not stay in England longer*] The English hedges and the New England stone walls; and I knew that I loved the stone walls best.

52 Neither Tilbury Town, nor any of the portrait-sketches, nor the "Town Down the River" referred to any particular place. In no instance whatever in any of his writing did he refer to anyone or any place. Tilbury Town might be any small New England small town.

53 The House on the Hill does not refer to any particular house that is or ever was, and surely not to a substantial stone house that is inhabited by the present Governor of the State. People who insist on identifying things or people in my poems are likely to go far astray.

54 I believe that genius can be stifled. It can be crushed.

[*"Rembrandt to Rembrandt" is*] a pretty good poem, . . . and one of [my] best.

[*Goethe's sense of being dictated to when he wrote his best verse*] I always do, in everything I write.

[*The onset of liberalism*] I am very glad that I shall not be alive twenty years from now.

55 I came to realize that a poet begins to live, if he lives at all, only after he is dead, and long ago ceased worrying about it.

56 I was lonely in my youth, and now I wish I could be.

[*Writing free verse*] No, I write badly enough as it is.

I don't think I have it in for women any more than the world has it in for them. Women are always either coming in for pity, or — I don't know what!

[*Lancelot's brutal treatment of Guinevere*] He had to!

[*While writing Tristram*] I slew T. and I. this morning. This afternoon I shall slay them again. Such love is not rare! It happens every day!

[*Percy MacKaye*] [He had] a sense of fun with no humor.

[*Shortening Lancelot by 500 lines*] I knew all the time I was going too far. My subconscious watchdog growled.

[*Roman Bartholow*] Nobody on earth would read it.

[*The Glory of the Nightingales*] But model citizens do not make good poems. It is full of sunshine, and there is only one suicide, which should make the reader feel warm and pleasant all over!

[*"Job the Rejected"*] I took it out of the oven too soon!

[*Failure of Talifer*] It is always dangerous to be different.

[*Short poems*] I can't do short ones. They don't come any more. I am not willing to publish inferior ones.

[*Van Zorn*] It is really a tragedy that opens trap-doors, and also gives glimpses of sun and stars.

[*Pulitzer Prize*] All prizes carry sort of a stigma.

57 Tennyson was a terrible ass.

[*Lancelot*] I find, in seeing the poem in the full flare of type, that I shall dispense with many of my experimental lines, and restore them, more or less, to the general metrical scheme of *Merlin* . . . . The long lines are all right, if read with the proper stress and speed, but I know well enough that I cannot count upon the attention and indulgence that such reading will require. Hence the knife.

[*Lancelot*] I wish . . . he [William Stanley Braithwaite] wouldn't find such world-shaking significance in the colors that Vivian put on to make Merlin take notice before she got tired of having him around. She may have been speaking in symbols, but I had never thought of that particular speech as anything more than a little sassy.

When I die, they ought to put D.D. — Defeated Dramatist — on my tombstone.

Hardy's blunder, both philosophic and artistic, was his reiteration of the idea of God jesting with mankind.

You know this sort of thing happens every day. I mean people love the way Tristram and Isolt were supposed to . . . It is not rare . . . It happens.

[*Tristram*] I am still in doubt as to some of the mushy parts, but I don't suppose that Isolt would call Tristram "Dear Sir," or that he would call her "Dear Madam." But I'll let it stand for the present. Now I'm set to go over the whole 4400 lines and see what I find. If it looks long to me, how is it going to look to others? I'm glad I don't know.

Sentimentality is far worse than death.

People ask me why I do not do the short poems any more. I can't. They don't come any more. At least, not good ones. And I'm not willing to publish poems I know are inferior to the early ones . . . . They don't come any more.

It's all I could have done, write poetry. I can't do anything else; I never could. And I have to write the kind of stuff I do write.

58 If you don't go with a brass band in front of you, they say you're a recluse.

I wrote sonnets because at the time I'd rather write sonnets than do anything else.

For two weeks I've gone to my studio every morning after breakfast, and stayed there till five o'clock. For two weeks I've searched for one word — and I haven't found it yet . . . . Today I removed the hyphen from hell-hound.

I set myself a definite time-limit to finish a piece of work, and I consider it as binding as a contract.

59 [*"Bokardo"*] I took a course in Logic once at Harvard. [Professor George Herbert] Palmer said the Bokardo was a figure which no one understood, and I took it as a symbol of the mystery of things.

[*Lancelot*] It is the most finished work, but I prefer *Merlin.* There are some better lines in it.

[*The Man Who Died Twice*] But there was a specific incident which started the thing in my mind. I was coming home one day in a trolley car on Staten Island and saw the sun setting, with a distant hill outlined against it, giving me a feeling of a precipice . . .

[*Dickens' Dombey and Son*] To me, *Dombey* ends with the death of little Paul.

[*Proust said the only reason artists struggle so hard is to repay in this existence a debt incurred in a previous one*] That comes nearer to being one hundred per cent true than anything I have heard in a long time.

60 If I could have only one book, do you know what I'd choose? . . . The dictionary! You've no idea how interesting it is to read just as one reads a book. It would last for years.

Bach is all right for you musicians and I know he is great. I just don't get much out of him.

[*Giuseppe Verdi*] I'm not ashamed of liking a good tune. His music will live long after a lot of the stuff these new fellows are turning out has been forgotten.

61 I suppose "Mr. Flood" is the best thing I ever did.

I wrote *Tristram* with my eye to the public.

[*Blank verse stories*] I can turn these things out once a year as long as they want me to.

62 [*Never gave readings*] I have enough trouble with private gatherings. For me a public platform would be nothing less than a public execution.

[*Exponents of the "new poetry"*] Most of them do not know how to write. They don't know what poetry is supposed to be or to do. Kipling knows it; so does Housman. Your friend Sandburg should have stayed in the army; he's all blood and guts. Amy Lowell might make real poetry out of her material, if she were a poet. Lindsay shouts a good sermon, but poetry is not a revival meeting. Your young poets are for the very young. Thank God I'm not one of them.

[*Miniver Cheevy, Eben Flood*] sustained by dreams and soothed by drink. I certainly should [know them]. I'm one of them.

Next time you see Clement Wood, tell him for me that Ben Trovato is not a man but a fairly common — I might say, well-found — Italian phrase.

63 People do not credit me with a sense of humor — and if my work means anything, it means that I have looked at the tragedies of life, and the tragedies of individuals, with a sense of humor.

NOTES

INTRODUCTION

1 Philip Butcher, editor, *The William Stanley Braithwaite Reader* (Ann Arbor, 1972), pp. 214-215. These remarks are taken from Braithwaite's "E.A. Robinson: 'Poor Devil, Poor Devil,'" one of the transcribed interviews taped for the Oral History Research Office of Columbia University in May 1956. In his *Edwin Arlington Robinson: A Biography* (New York, 1938), p. 325, Hermann Hagedorn gives his version of this story with some variance in details of time and place.

2 December 14, 1920, in Ridgely Torrence, editor, *Selected Letters of Edwin Arlington Robinson* (New York, 1940), pp. 122-123.

3 December 16, 1921, *ibid.*, p. 128.

4 January 22, 1921, in Richard Cary, editor, *Edwin Arlington Robinson's Letters to Edith Brower* (Cambridge, Mass., 1968), p. 177.

5 See his remarks, of speckled particularity, in the notes to the following poems in this volume: "For a Copy of Poe's Poems," "The Miracle," "For a Book by Thomas Hardy," "The Children of the Night," "Boston," "For Calderon," "Walt Whitman," "A Poem for Max Nordau," "The Night Before," "Octave (Saints of all times)," "Octaves, I," "Romance," "Twilight Song," "Au Revoir," "Modred." David Brown's study of "Some Rejected Poems of Edwin Arlington Robinson," *American Literature*, VII (January 1936), 395-414, was done before most of Robinson's letters were accessible. Brown examined the discarded poems from *The Torrent and The Night Before* and *The Children of the Night*, condemning their defects on the basis of Robinson's longer-run tone, techniques, diction, and themes.

6 To Edith Brower, December 11, 1921, in Cary, p. 179.

7 Ellsworth Barnard, *Edwin Arlington Robinson: A Critical Study* (New York, 1952), p. 276, n. 25.

8 Harry Salpeter, "E.A. Robinson, Poet," New York *World* (May 15, 1927), 8M.

9 Alice Hunt Bartlett, "The Dynamics of American Poetry—III," *Poetry Review*, XV (January-February 1924), 36.

10 December 7, 1896, in Denham Sutcliffe, editor, *Untriangulated Stars: Letters of Edwin Arlington Robinson to Harry DeForest Smith 1890-1905* (Cambridge, Mass., 1947), p. 265.

11 Lucius Beebe, "Dignified Faun: A Portrait of E.A.R.," *Outlook*, CLV (August 27, 1930), 649.

12 Hagedorn, p. 47; Emery Neff, *Edwin Arlington Robinson* (New York, 1948), pp. 89-90. In *Colby Library Quarterly*, VIII (September 1969), 387, Peter Dechert confirms that "it was written by [Alanson Tucker] Schumann, and published under his name in the Gardiner *Reporter-Journal*."

13 To compare texts see *The Globe,* IV (September 1894), 828, or Charles Beecher Hogan, *A Bibliography of Edwin Arlington Robinson* (New Haven, 1936), p. 100, for "The House on the Hill"; Sutcliffe, pp. 19-20, for "Horace to Leuconoë."

14 Hagedorn, p. 32; Laura E. Richards, *E.A.R.* (Cambridge, Mass., 1936), p. 25.

15 Richards, p. 15.

16 October 11, 1891, in Sutcliffe, p. 31.

17 Daniel Gregory Mason, "Early Letters of Edwin Arlington Robinson: First Series," *Virginia Quarterly Review,* XIII (Winter 1937), 60. The asterisk after "shards" is footnoted: *June-bugs. *E.A.R.*

18 Louis Untermeyer, *From Another World* (New York, 1939), p. 226.

19 Louis Untermeyer, "E.A.R.: A Remembrance," *Saturday Review,* XLVIII (April 10, 1965), 34. See also Carty Ranck's version of this story in his "Edwin Arlington Robinson," New York *Herald Tribune Magazine* (December 14, 1930), 9.

20 July 28, 1911, in Torrence, p. 71.

21 Carl Van Doren, "Post-War: The Literary Twenties," *Harper's,* CLXXIII (July 1936), 154.

22 Untermeyer, *SR,* p. 33.

23 Beebe, p. 647, Beebe's delineation is one of the most winsome and instructive: "A reticent Corinthian, combining the shyness of a Verlaine and the superior aloofness of Thomas Hardy . . . . A mildly dignified faun in rimless spectacles, he shuns the deadly testimonial dinner as though he had once experienced the hospitality of the Borgias, and he is a complete stranger to the woman's clubs and lecture platforms so beloved of the trained seal order of litterateurs."

24 Theodore Maynard, "Edwin Arlington Robinson," *Catholic World,* CXLI (June 1935), 269.

25 Untermeyer, *SR,* p. 33.

POEMS

THALIA

Robinson's first published poem, from *The Reporter Monthly,* I (March 29, 1890), [3], a four-page Literary Supplement of the *Kennebec Reporter;* reprinted in Charles Beecher Hogan, *A Bibliography of Edwin Arlington Robinson* (Yale University Press: New Haven, 1936), p. 167, and in facsimile facing the title page.

PALAEMON—DAMOETAS—MENALCAS

From Ridgely Torrence, editor, *Selected Letters of Edwin Arlington Robinson* (Macmillan Company: New York, 1940), pp. 181-184.

Torrence transcribed this translation of Virgil's "Eclogue III" from the nine-page copy Robinson sent with a letter to Arthur R. Gledhill on April 17, 1890. The date "Nov. 1889" is affixed to the end of the verses. Robinson wrote: "You will find it rather close [Torrence read "loose"] for an attempt at poetical translation. . . . You will notice the body of the thing to be in pentameters while the singing match is in Alexandrine couplets — as I wished to retain the appearance of the original as much as possible" (Torrence, p. 3).

Torrence's rendition of Robinson's manuscript is lamentable. He departs from Robinson's preferred punctuation in over thirty instances and transforms the following:

Lines	*Torrence*	*Robinson*
2, 5	Argon	Aegon
5	Naera	Neaira
15	Ulycon	Mycon
17	Daphne's	Daphnis
30	one	me
34	Lo!	So;
74	muses	Muses
75	Ulysses	Muse
96	Amaryllis	Amarylis
99, 103	Pollis	Pollio
104	bramble	brambles
117	held	hold
127	drunk	drank

In line 55 Torrence simply omits Robinson's "soft" before "acanthus." (Letter and manuscript in Harvard College Library)

Robinson reversed Virgil's subtitle, "Menalcas—Damoetas—Palaemon"; used 127 lines in his adaptation, sixteen more than Virgil; spelled proper names to his own taste; spoke of "Dryads," unmentioned by Virgil; substituted "Muses" for "Camenae" and "mountain Muses" for "Pierides."

In his copy of P. Virgilii Maronis, *Opera*, Interpretatione et Notis by Carolus Ruaeus (H.C. Carey & J. Lea: Philadelphia, 1825), Robinson made twelve pencil notations in the margins or above words he underlined in "Eclogue III," suggesting meanings in English. He did not go beyond the first twenty lines. (In Colby College Library)

On August 16, 1924 Robinson expostulated to Laura E. Richards: "Poetry cannot be translated anyhow" (Torrence, p. 138).

THE CLAM-DIGGER: CAPITOL ISLAND

From *The Reporter Monthly*, I (April 26, 1890), [2]; reprinted in *Colby Library Quarterly*, X (December 1974), 505. This poem has not before been noted or attributed to Robinson by his bibliographers. It is in point of order his second published poem. See Richard Cary, " 'The Clam-Digger: Capitol Island': A Robinson Sonnet Recovered," in *CLQ*.

ISAAC PITMAN

From *The Phonographic World*, V (May 1890), 280; reprinted in *Our Phonographic Poets*, compiled by "Topsy Typist" [Enoch Newton Minor], (Popular Publishing Company; New York, 1904), pp. 79-80; in *The Colophon*, n.s. III (Summer 1938), 359-360; and in William White, *Edwin Arlington Robinson: A Supplementary Bibliography* (Kent State University Press: Kent, Ohio, 1971), pp. 119-120, the last two with minor differences.

The date "March 21, 1890" is affixed to the end of the poem in the original printing. Shortly after finishing high school Robinson took some lessons in stenography.

See Charles Beecher Hogan, "A Poet at the Phonic Shrine," in *The Colophon* for an account of the re-emergence of this poem.

THE GALLEY RACE

From *The Reporter Monthly*, I (May 31, 1890), [3]; reprinted in Charles Beecher Hogan, *A Bibliography of Edwin Arlington Robinson* (Yale University Press: New Haven, 1936), pp. 167-173, with [*sic*] interpolated in three places to indicate typographical errors in the newspaper version.

Robinson takes 197 lines to render Virgil's 182; omits Virgil's direct references to Phaëthon, Cori, Syrtibus, Maleaeque, Nereidum Phorcique, Maeandro, Phegeus Sagarisque, Minerva; substitutes "Trojans" for Aeneadas, Dardana, Teucri; "Nymphs" for Nereids, and "Ganymede" for "sublimem pedibus."

On April 17, 1890 Robinson wrote Arthur R. Gledhill: "Yesterday I finished a translation (blank verse) of the 'Galley Race', Book V, 104-285 . . . . Great sport but devilish hard work . . . . I worked two days on two lines — that is to say, it was two days before I decided. This was the place:

> *—Illa Noto citius volucrique sagitta*
> *Ad terram fugit et portu se condidit alto.* 242-243
>
> *"Swift as the wind, in arrowy flight she speeds*
> *And rides triumphant in the land-locked port."*
> (Torrence, p. 3)

TRIOLET

From Hermann Hagedorn, *Edwin Arlington Robinson: A Biography* (Macmillan Company: New York, 1938), p. 47.

Hagedorn errs in the chronology of this poem, placing it between 1887-1889. On March 11, 1891 Robinson wrote Arthur R. Gledhill: "By the way I made a triolet yesterday; here it is: [the poem follows]. Observe the bucolic pathos and fine feeling. This form of verse is of French extraction and if you ever study old French literature you will probably come across hosts of them. They give a man a chance to pour out his whole soul (as I have done) in eight lines" (Harvard College Library).

BALLADE OF A SHIP

From Edwin Arlington Robinson, *The Children of the Night* (Richard G. Badger & Company: Boston, 1897), pp. 18-19. Originally published as "Ballade of the White Ship" in *Harvard Advocate*, LII (October 16, 1891), 22; reprinted with changes in capitalization, spelling, punctuation, and italics in the pirated *Three Poems By Edwin Arlington Robinson* (Cambridge, 1928); and in Donald Hall, editor, *The Harvard Advocate Anthology* (Twayne Publishers, Inc.: New York, 1950), pp. 53-54.

Robinson included the poem in *The Torrent and The Night Before* (1896), pp. 6-7, with revised title and verbal changes in these lines:

1 Down they went to the still, green water—
4 And out they sailed on the silvering bay:
5 The quick ship flew on her roystering way,
9 'Twas a king's gay son with a king's gay daughter
11 Hurrying on to the lone, cold slaughter
19 The ravenous reef in his hard clutch caught her
20 And whirled her down where the dead men stay—
22 The shrieks and curses of mad souls dying.
25 Prince, do you sleep 'mid the perishing clay
26 To the mournful dirge of the sea-birds' crying?
27 Or does blood still quicken and steel still slay—

Robinson also altered some end-line punctuation and omitted "L'Envoi" before the final stanza. Line 13 was inadvertently omitted at the top of page 7 (Robinson filling it in by hand on a number of his presentation copies). In *The Children of the Night* (1897) he restored line 13 and "Envoy" before the final stanza. Of the missing line he wrote Edith Brower on May 15, 1897: "I don't care much for the poem, but I would rather have it printed as it was written. It was bad enough then" (Richard Cary, editor, *Edwin Arlington Robinson's Letters to Edith Brower* [Cambridge, Mass., 1968], p. 45).

IN HARVARD 5

From *Harvard Advocate*, LII (December 11, 1891), 85; reprinted in the pirated *Three Poems By Edwin Arlington Robinson* (Cambridge, 1928), where line 10 begins "Their spirits" instead of "Thin spirits"; and in Donald Hall, editor, *The Harvard Advocate Anthology* (Twayne Publishers, Inc.: New York, 1950), pp. 55-56.

On December 8, 1891 Robinson spoke of "my latest poetical (?) effusion, — a rondeau entitled 'In Harvard 5.' The subject is Shakespeare . . . " (Denham Sutcliffe, editor, *Untriangulated Stars: Letters of Edwin Arlington Robinson to Harry DeForest Smith 1890-1905* [Harvard University Press: Cambridge, 1947], p. 45). Harvard 5 was the lecture hall used by Professor Francis J. Child for his course on Shakespeare.

MENOETES

From *Harvard Advocate,* LIII (March 15, 1892), 32; reprinted in Charles Livingstone Stebbins, editor, *Harvard Lyrics* (Brown and Company: Boston, 1899), p. 111, with "overthrown" instead of "thrown" in line 9.

This sonnet is based on the incident in Virgil's *Aeneid,* Book V, lines 166-182. Robinson translated lines 104-285 of Book V as "The Galley Race," reproduced in this volume.

BALLADE OF DEAD MARINERS: ENVOI

From Denham Sutcliffe, editor, *Untriangulated Stars: Letters of Edwin Arlington Robinson to Harry DeForest Smith 1890-1905* (Harvard University Press: Cambridge, 1947), p. 111.

In his letter of October 5, 1893 Robinson says to Smith: "I suppose I shall have to write a 'Ballade of Dead Mariners.' The idea, with three or four others, has been chasing me for some time, and I know of but one way to get rid of them — write them out. Even that doesn't always do it, but one feels better after making a trial. Here is the 'envoi' as it came to me of a sudden: [the envoi follows]. This is in the rough, and may be changed more or less. I never tried one in decasyllables before, but I think I shall like [it] as well as the popular eight-syllable form. The things may not be worth the trouble of the making, but there is a fascination about them that I cannot get over" (pp. 111-112). No evidence has yet turned up that Robinson completed or published this ballade.

DOUBTS

From Denham Sutcliffe, editor, *Untriangulated Stars: Letters of Edwin Arlington Robinson to Harry DeForest Smith 1890-1905* (Harvard University Press: Cambridge, 1947), p. 146.

On April 22, 1894 Robinson wrote to Smith: I have written a queer poem, but I haven't the nerve to send it to you yet. It needs a little revision before [being] subjected to even the most friendly criticism, and it is in this little revision that my difficulty lies. The whole thing — forty lines — was written between twelve and one o'clock while I was waiting for my dinner, and has an air of unsatisfactory completeness about it which I am at a loss to overcome. When I fix it, I shall send you a copy — yes, I will send you two stanzas now while I am talking about it: [the stanzas follow]. I call the thing 'Doubts.' The stanzas quoted are the fifth and sixth out of ten. I think that there is at least a straightforwardness — what a devil of a word that is! — about the poem, which you will like. There is nothing artificial, and, I fear, little intelligible; but for all that I rather think you will like it better than the 'House on the Hill.' As for myself, I think I prefer the villanelle" (p. 146). No evidence has yet turned up of publication beyond this fragment.

FOR A COPY OF POE'S POEMS

From *Lippincott's Magazine,* LXXVIII (August 1906) 243; reprinted in *Edwin Arlington Robinson, A Collection of His Works From the Library of Bacon Collamore* (Privately printed: Hartford, 1936), p. 14.

Robinson's letter to Harry Smith makes it clear that he had submitted this poem to the *Dial* some time before June 17, 1894 (Sutcliffe, *Untriangulated Stars*, p. 166). After intermittent fretting he reported on February 3, 1895: "The editor of *Lippincott's Magazine* . . . sent me a check for seven dollars . . . . I fixed up the sonnet a little before I sent it on, so they did not get it just as the *Dial* people saw it — if they ever did that. The third line now reads 'Bleak and unblossomed were the ways he knew,' which seems to have some jingle and a little strength" (p. 203).

Elated by his new-found professional status, he told Smith on March 10, 1895: "Think I may as well stop now and wait till the Lippincotts print my 'Poe' " (p. 215), a grim irony in view of the fact that the poem was filed away for eleven and a half years. By April 2, 1895 he was "honestly" considering it "a very poor thing" and wincing "when anyone mentions the subject in my presence" (Edwin S. Fussell, *Edwin Arlington Robinson: The Literary Background of a Traditional Poet* [Berkeley, 1954], p. 17).

Thoroughly disillusioned, he wrote Edith Brower on June 6, 1897: "Two years ago its appearance would have tickled me, but I have grown old since then and would not give five cents to see it now. In fact, I am not entirely sure that I would not rather have him keep it pigeonholed for good; there are places in it that don't suit me at all, though I fancy the sestet is tolerable" (Cary, *EAR Letters*, p. 48).

THE MIRACLE

From Edwin Arlington Robinson, *The Children of the Night* (Richard G. Badger & Company: Boston, 1897), p. 58. Originally published in *The Globe*, IV (September 1894), 829; reprinted in *The Torrent and The Night Before* (1896), p. 18, with several changes in punctuation, removal of capital letters from "pity," "forgiveness," "autumn," and "spring," and substitution of "love" for "Faith" in line 14. Robinson indicates that the sonnet was also reprinted in the New York *Sun* (Sutcliffe, *Untriangulated Stars*, pp. 233-234).

On October 7, 1894 Robinson wrote Smith: "The 'long awaited,' that is *The Globe* has come . . . The proof reader evidently has his own ideas of punctuation, but aside from that they (the poems) are printed quite to my satisfaction. The matter that troubles me most is the question whether they are worth printing or not. Sometimes I rather think they are, then I think they are not. I can only tell by looking at them five years from now. That generally settles such matters" (p. 170). The other poem in this issue of *The Globe* was "The House on the Hill," which Robinson admitted to *Collected Poems*.

TAVERN SONGS: CHORUS

From Denham Sutcliffe, editor, *Untriangulated Stars: Letters of Edwin Arlington Robinson to Harry DeForest Smith 1890-1905* (Harvard University Press: Cambridge, 1947), p. 170.

In his letter of October 7, 1894 Robinson said to Smith: "I am going to write some 'Tavern Songs' this winter . . . . This chorus will give you some idea of what they will be like: [the chorus follows]. I shall endeavor to put a little mysticism in them, and make them worth while as literature; at the same time trying to make them musical enough in themselves to be songs first and poems after. Of course I may not write them at all but I hope to do a few, at least" (p. 170). A year later: "I have the music all settled for a ballad, which, I trust will some day be a Tavern Song" (p. 233). On December 14, 1895: "The 'Tavern' part of my book is not like anything I ever wrote before and I doubt much if I ever try anything like it again. The songs have been for the most part villainously hard to make" (p. 238).

Robinson did include a group of tavern songs (among them "Luke Havergal," "John Evereldown," "Edward Alphabet") in the manuscript of *The Torrent and The Night Before*, which he initially named *The Tavern and The Night Before.* After the second rejection, he changed the title and cancelled most of the songs.

THE *ANTIGONE* OF SOPHOCLES

From Denham Sutcliffe, editor, *Untriangulated Stars: Letters of Edwin Arlington Robinson to Harry DeForest Smith 1890-1905* (Harvard University Press: Cambridge, 1947), pp. [1] 167, [2] 175-176, [3] 177, [4] 179, [5] 182-185.

Robinson first suggested "a metrical translation of the *Antigone*" to Smith on February 4, 1894 as "a little scheme for this summer." "You might find pleasure and profit in writing out a correct prose version of the play, keeping the Greek spirit as much as possible, and in guiding me in the choice of words and suggestions as to the classical effect of my verses. My choice would be to make it in the main unrhymed, depending upon sonority and picturesqueness for the effect." He thought "An edition of fifty copies printed for private circulation," with both their names on the title page, though "a kind of a Spanish castle in Greece," might not be inconceivable (Sutcliffe, p. 125). Smith consented, began sending his prose version in batches, writing "Finis" to his end of the project on December 13, 1894.

Robinson declared that he did not "intend to attempt anything like a reproduction of the Greek metres — my idea is merely to suggest a little of the original form to the American eye — thus preserving an ocular resemblance between the translation and the Greek text" (p. 134). He worked less consistently than Smith, sometimes calling for more copy quickly, yet struggling with the text as late as November 26, 1895. The graph of Robinson's ups and downs with the *Antigone* may be traced in his letters *passim*, pp. 125-283.

Smith's prose rendition, with some notations in Robinson's hand, is now in Colby College Library. Robinson scribbled two fragments on this manuscript which are not included in Sutcliffe:

I, too the stormy son of Dryas
For his unyielding anger was entombed
By Bacchus in a rocky cave; and there
The splendid recklessness of his mad life
Trickles and ebbs away. He knew too late
That in his madness he had
Touched a god
With fiery words: for that was his design
[lines 955-961]

There is no happiness for any man
If that man be not wise; but he must hold
With things that are appointed of the gods
With might but reverence. For in old age,
When wisdom comes at last, his flaunted words
Are paid back with intolerable blows.
[lines 1345-1352]

In his *Colophon* essay, "The First Seven Years" (reproduced in this volume), Robinson states that the manuscript of his metrical translation "disappeared mysteriously." James Notopoulos in "Sophocles *and Captain Craig*," *New England Quarterly*, XVII (March 1944), 109, says that Smith believed it "was later destroyed by the poet."

KOSMOS

From Edwin Arlington Robinson, *The Children of the Night* (Richard G. Badger & Company: Boston, 1897), p. 43. Originally published in *The Globe*, V (October 1895), 407; reprinted in *The Torrent and The Night Before* (1896), p. 32, with several changes in punctuation, removal of capital letters from "he" in line 5, and from "love" in line 12. The lower case "h" in line 5 may be an unnoticed typographical error, for see line 8. In *The Children* Robinson added one dash and deleted three.

Robinson to Harry Smith, October 6, 1895: " 'Kosmos' . . . is crazier than ['The Miracle']. You heard me read the first draft of it — which was not much like its present form — and did not care a damn for it. I doubt if you like it any better this time" (Sutcliffe, p. 234).

FOR A BOOK BY THOMAS HARDY

From Edwin Arlington Robinson, *The Children of the Night* (Richard G. Badger & Company: Boston, 1897), p. 56. Originally published in *The Critic*, XXIV (November 23, 1895), 348, with the footnote "Written before the appearance of 'Hearts Insurgent.' " (This was the title of the serial version of *Jude the Obscure* which ran in *Harper's New Monthly Magazine*, December 1894-November 1895.) The sonnet was reprinted in *The Torrent and The Night Before* (1896), pp. 20-21, with no verbal changes. In *The Children* Robinson omitted the comma at end of line 13.

Robinson mailed a presentation copy of *The Torrent and The Night Before* to Hardy but there is no record that he responded.

Sensitive to the views of a few people he trusted, Robinson wrote to Edith Brower on April 21, 1897: "I am always glad for intelligent 'damnation.' I have been lucky enough to get a little of it — enough to make me ready to cancel the Hardy sonnet" (Cary, *EAR Letters*, p. 39). And Carl Van Doren hypothesized: "I never asked him why he dropped it, but from my acquaintance with him I should say it was because he later felt he had spoken somewhat melodramatically, and it was more obviously personal than he liked to be" (Carl J. Weber, "The Cottage Lights of Wessex," *Colby Mercury*, VI [February 1936], 65).

EDWARD ALPHABET

From Denham Sutcliffe, editor, *Untriangulated Stars: Letters of Edwin Arlington Robinson to Harry DeForest Smith 1890-1905* (Harvard University Press: Cambridge, 1947), p. 238. Originally published in Hermann Hagedorn, *Edwin Arlington Robinson; A Biography* (Macmillan Company: New York, 1938), p. 96, with some differences in punctuation, a transposition ("ever he can") in line 3, and the statement that Robinson wrote this tavern song as "a diversion from metaphysics."

Hagedorn (p. 389) wrongly asserts that "The jingle about Edward Alphabet has survived only because the memory of Professor Harry de Forest Smith gave it lodging." Sutcliffe transcribed the quatrain from Robinson's letter of December 14, 1895, where he remarked: "My songs are corkers — particularly Edward Alphabet: [the poem follows] and so forth. You may not think it from the first lines but the poem is an argument against the present attitude of the females" (p. 238).

THE CHILDREN OF THE NIGHT

From Edwin Arlington Robinson, *The Children of the Night* (Richard G. Badger & Company: Boston, 1897), pp. 11-12. Originally published in the Boston *Evening Transcript* (January 4, 1896), 4; reprinted in *The Torrent and The Night Before* (1896), pp. 26-27, where Robinson substituted "other" for "better" in stanza 3, line 1 and "sky" for "night" in stanza 10, line 4; capitalized "Him" in stanza 8, line 4 (evidently a typographical error, for see stanza 9, line 3). In *The Children* he made several changes in punctuation and substituted "imbittered" for "embittered" in stanza 4, line 3.

Robinson said of the poem that he "was painting the front fence when the thing came so fast that I had to go into the house and write it down" (Hagedorn, p. 101). As for its omission from his *Collected Poems*, he wrote Edith Brower, "all I can say is that it was left out because it seemed to be rather young and futile, and because the same thing was said again in the latter part of 'The Man Against the Sky'" (Cary, *EAR Letters*, p. 179). See also Ellsworth Barnard, *Edwin Arlington Robinson: A Critical Study* (New York, 1952), p. 275, n. 25, where Robinson calls it "naive and juvenile"; and Lucius Beebe, *Aspects of the Poetry of Edwin Arlington Robinson* (Cambridge, Mass., 1928), pp. 18-19, where he sees it as "too boyish to go on the permanent record." On May 28, 1927 he wrote: "I omitted 'The Children of the Night' from my *Collected Poems* in the hope of exterminating it." (Richard Cary, *Early Reception of Edwin Arlington Robinson: The First Twenty Years* [Waterville, Maine, 1974], p. 69).

"I MAKE NO MEASURE OF THE WORDS THEY SAY"

From *The Globe,* VI (May 1896), 143-144; reprinted in Charles Beecher Hogan, *A Bibliography of Edwin Arlington Robinson* (Yale University Press: New Haven, 1936), p. 173.

In his letter of April 17, 1892, while attending Harvard, Robinson told Harry Smith: "I have made a little verse today, however — part of a sonnet beginning:

I make no measure of the words they say
  Who come with snaky tongues to me and tell
  Of all the woe awaiting me in Hell
When from this goodly world I go my way, etc.

Eventually I shall go on to say how the appearance of a good wholesome white-haired man who never told a lie or drank Maine whiskey impresses me, and how I draw a lesson from the unspoken sermon of his own self and realize the real magnificence of better things — the which I have an idea will make the closing line. I shall spring it on the *Advocate*. They may object to the morality of it, though, and throw it out (Sutcliffe, pp. 59-60).

For a discussion of Robinson's conception of this poem see Edwin S. Fussell, *Edwin Arlington Robinson: The Literary Background of a Traditional Poet* (Berkeley, 1954), pp. 171-173.

BOSTON (sestet)

From Edwin Arlington Robinson, *The Children of the Night* (Richard G. Badger & Company: Boston, 1897), p. 51. Originally published as a sonnet in the Boston *Evening Transcript* (October 8, 1896), 6; reprinted in *The Torrent and The Night Before* (1896), pp. 33-34, with some changes in punctuation. In *The Children* Robinson made a trifling change in punctuation. He selected only the octave for inclusion in his *Collected Poems*.

Of the whole poem he wrote Harry Smith: "Ever since I lied so like the devil about 'my northern pines' I have had visions of Auckland" (Sutcliffe, p. 287); and to Edith Brower, "I was referred to the other evening, here in Cambridge, as a fellow who wrote 'a corking good thing on a man who shot himself, and a rotten sonnet on Boston!'" (Cary, *EAR Letters*, p. 89).

FOR SOME POEMS BY MATTHEW ARNOLD

From Edwin Arlington Robinson, *The Children of the Night* (Richard G. Badger & Company: Boston, 1897), p. 41. Originally published in *The Torrent and The Night Before* (1896), p. 11, with one difference in punctuation.

BALLADE OF DEAD FRIENDS

From Edwin Arlington Robinson, *The Children of the Night* (Richard G. Badger & Company: Boston, 1897), pp. 24-25. Originally published in *The Torrent and The Night Before* (1896), pp. 18-19, as "The Ballade of Dead Friends," with five variants in punctuation and "eying" spelled "eyeing" in stanza 3, line 5.

Date of composition may be judged from Robinson's letter to Harry Smith on November 26, 1894, in which he reports "I have written" the poem (Sutcliffe, p. 188). When Edmund Clarence Stedman selected this ballade for inclusion in his *An American Anthology, 1787-1899* (Boston, 1900), Robinson chaffed about his "somewhat lugubrious admiration" (Cary, *EAR Letters*, p. 130).

FOR CALDERON

From Edwin Arlington Robinson, *The Torrent and The Night Before* (Printed for the Author: Cambridge, Mass., 1896), pp. 22-24.

This is one of the two poems Robinson did not carry over into *The Children of the Night* (1897); the other, "A Poem for Max Nordau." While considering the contents for his second book he said tentatively to Edith Brower on April 21, 1897, "[I] feel very shaky about 'For Calderon' — which always seemed to me a little childish"; then definitively on September 7, "I have thrown out 'For Calderon . . . ' (Cary, *EAR Letters*, pp. 39, 56). Later he wrote her: "I have something the same objection to ['The Night Before'] that I had for 'Calderon' which was off the same piece and done in the same mechanical way" (p. 82).

THE WORLD

From Edwin Arlington Robinson, *The Children of the Night* (Richard G. Badger & Company: Boston, 1897), p. 16. Originally published in *The Torrent and The Night Before* (1896), pp. 25-26, without the capital letter in "Paradise," stanza 2, line 2.

WALT WHITMAN

From Edwin Arlington Robinson, *The Children of the Night* (Richard G. Badger & Company: Boston, 1897), p. 85. Originally published in *The Torrent and The Night Before* (1896), pp. 31-32, with three differences in punctuation.

Robinson wrote to Walter Hubbell on December 16, 1896: "You will find the gist of [my philosophy] in the 'Two Sonnets' and in the last section of 'Walt Whitman' " (John William Pye, editor, *Edwin Arlington Robinson: A Bio-Bibliography* [Hartford, 1971], p. 3). Many years later he said: "I was very young when I wrote it, but I knew all the time I was writing it that I didn't really mean it" (Winfield Townley Scott, "To See Robinson," *New Mexico Quarterly*, XXVI [Summer 1956], 176).

A POEM FOR MAX NORDAU

From Edwin Arlington Robinson, *The Torrent and The Night Before* (Printed for the Author: Cambridge, Mass., 1896), p. 33.

This is one of the two poems Robinson did not carry over into *The Children of the Night* (1897); the other, "For Calderon." On September 7, 1897 he said conclusively to Edith Brower: "I have thrown out . . . 'Max Nordau' (Cary, *EAR Letters*, p. 56). Laura E. Richards wrote: "His reason for rejecting this poem was that it was meant to be funny, and he was afraid people might not realize this" (*E.A.R.* [Cambridge, Mass., 1936], pp. 57-58) after Robinson's comment that "This is the difficulty (or possibly the vital advantage) of being born a comedian under the wrong (or again possibly the best) conditions" (p. 55).

THE NIGHT BEFORE

From Edwin Arlington Robinson, *The Children of the Night* (Richard G. Badger & Company: Boston, 1897), pp. 71-84. Originally published in *The Torrent and The Night Before* (1896), pp. 34-44. Robinson made more numerous revisions in this poem than was usual with him. Trying no doubt to affect pace and stress, he eliminated or shifted scores of commas, dashes, and three-dot series; in the same quest, eliminated two stanzaic indentations and separated a third with six dots. He also changed "Domine" to "Dominie" in lines 1, 6, 19, 359; capitalized "heaven" in line 153, "his" in line 72; respelled "marvelous" in line 367. He let slip the typographical error "When loves goes" which had not occurred before in line 210. He dropped the definite article from "But the scenes" in line 180, but his only alterations of solid import were to discard the epigraph, "As if God made him and then wondered why," and turn the ending of line 38, "Not one of those little black lawyers were told it" to "had guessed it."

From the start, Robinson's feelings toward this poem were tenuous. On October 28, 1896 to Arthur R. Gledhill: " 'The Night Before' is an attempt to be absolutely impersonal which, of course, is an impossibility" (Torrence, *Selected Letters*, p. 13). On February 3, 1897 to Harry Smith: " 'The Night Before' is purely objective, and may be called anything from pessimism to rot. I must confess that I haven't the slightest idea whether it is good for anything or not. I printed it to find out; but the opinions I have received are so conflicting that I am not much better off than I was before . . . . I am afraid it is one of those unfortunate narrative pieces which require a second reading before it amounts to anything at all" (Sutcliffe, pp. 273-274). On August 25, 1898 to Edith Brower: "[Dante Gabriel Rossetti's] The 'Last Confession' partly suggested 'The Night Before,' but I was not conscious of it at the time of writing six or eight years ago. It was partly a 'job' done entirely with cold blood and consciously for literary practice. This may account for some rather inflammatory passages in it, which I had hardly written had the thing been done more spontaneously . . . . It is about the only thing in the book that is absolutely impersonal, but still I have never been altogether glad that I have printed it. I have something the same objection to it that I had for 'Calderon 'which was off the same piece and done in the same mechanical way" (Cary, *EAR Leters*, p. 82).

On several occasions between May 27, 1894 and February, 1897 Robinson discussed the poem in detail with Harry Smith. See Sutcliffe, pp. 158-159, 161-162, 163, 165, 238, 264-265, 273.

SHOOTING STARS

From *The Globe, VI* (December 1896), 391; reprinted in Charles Beecher Hogan, *A Bibliography of Edwin Arlington Robinson* (Yale University Press: New Haven, 1936), pp. 173-174.

OCTAVE (Saints of all times)

From Boston *Evening Transcript* (February 26, 1897), 6; reprinted in Charles Beecher Hogan, *A Bibliography of Edwin Arlington Robinson* (Yale University Press: New Haven, 1936), pp. 174-175.

Robinson to Edith Brower on March 14, 1897: "I take the liberty to throw in a clipping from the Boston *Transcript* which reveals a rather startling typographical 'error' " (Cary, *EAR Letters,* p. 30). The phrase "all the tomes" in the last line is crossed over and "any tons" written below. Brower pasted this to page 44 of her copy of *The Torrent and The Night Before,* now in Colby College Library.

On April 10, 1897 Robinson wrote her: "The [octave] from the *Transcript* is altogether too rickety to be considered for a moment as a finished poem, though I don't know just what I can do with it." By September 7 he had decided. "I have also thrown away the 'Saints of all Times' octave. Couldn't make it go to suit me. Sometime I may straighten it out, but rather doubt it" (pp. 37, 56).

THE IDEALIST

From Richard Cary, editor, *Edwin Arlington Robinson's Letters to Edith Brower* (Harvard University Press: Cambridge, 1968), p. 36. Originally published in *Colby Library Quarterly,* II (February 1947), 13, and reprinted in William White, *Edwin Arlington Robinson: A Supplementary Bibliography* (Kent State University Press: Kent, Ohio, 1971), p. 137, under the title "[Idealist?: An Octave]," with a comma at end of line 1 and "Take these" instead of "Take them" in line 6.

As a postscript to Edith Brower on April 2, 1897 Robinson wrote: "Here is another Octave:—" and copied down this poem for her (Cary, p. 36).

While compiling the contents for *The Children of the Night* (1897) Robinson wrote Miss Brower:" 'The Idealist' won't suit it. There wasn't enough to the thing to make it worth printing" (Cary, p. 56).

TWO OCTAVES

From Edwin Arlington Robinson, *The Children of the Night* (Richard G. Badger & Company: Boston, 1897), pp. 36-37.

OCTAVES I, III

From Edwin Arlington Robinson, *The Children of the Night* (Richard G. Badger & Company: Boston, 1897), pp. 91, 93. Of the twenty-five octaves in this edition, Robinson retained only twenty-three in his *Collected Poems.*

On April 1, 1914 he appealed to Edith Brower: "please don't quote that incriminating first 'Octave,' which is a little the worst thing that I have done — and that is saying much" (Cary, *EAR Letters*, p. 156).

ROMANCE

From Edwin Arlington Robinson, *The Children of the Night* (Richard G. Badger & Company: Boston, 1897), pp. 118-119; Part I reprinted in Richard Cary, editor, *Edwin Arlington Robinson's Letters to Edith Brower* (Harvard University Press: Cambridge, 1968), p. 43.

As a postscript to Miss Brower on May 9, 1897 Robinson wrote "Quatrain—" and copied down "Boys" for her (p. 43). In his next letter, May 15, he said, "The 'Brothers' was another wicked grind. A year ago it was a sonnet; now I'm not sure that it is anything" (p. 45).

In the second letter he also said: " 'J. Wetherell' was an 'inspiration'; and is about on the level I think with the bulk of inspirational work. The first draught comes easily, then comes the struggle." On June 27 he called it "As far as I know . . . . the best thing I have done," by which he meant "from the point of view of mere art: the thought . . . 'isn't exactly transcendental' " (p. 52). On September 7 he decreed that " 'James Wetherell' is going to be one of them" [poems in *The Children of the Night*] (p. 56).

LIMERICKS

[1] from *Virginia Quarterly Review*, XXXI (Winter 1937), 63; [2] and [3] from Richard Cary, editor, *Edwin Arlington Robinson's Letters to Edith Brower* (Harvard University Press: Cambridge, 1968), pp. 147, 148.

[1] appears in a letter to Daniel Gregory Mason marked "[Undated]," which he positions between letters dated May 7 and May 31, 1900. Internal evidence places the letter sometime after October 1899. Robinson told Mason: "Remember too that there is always the appalling possibility of sonnets and Calm Limericks. This is a Calm Limerick: [it follows]. Sabattis is a town in Maine. I have never been there, but I know it must be a calm place" (pp. 63-64).

[2] appears in Robinson's letter of July 8, 1902. "This is what I learn in Cambridge," he added wryly.

[3] appears in Robinson's letter of October 13, 1902.

PLUMMER STREET, GARDINER, MAINE

From *American Literature*, XXIII (May 1951), 178-179.

This poem appears in Robinson's letter to William Vaughn Moody of May 10, 1900. Robinson said: "Speaking of circuses, here is a sonnet for you:— [it follows]. This is not just in my line, but I send it along, thinking you may get a kind of reminiscent satisfaction from it. I fancy it is not an 'object of art.' "

TWILIGHT SONG

Published in facsimile: Richard Cary, editor, *Edwin Arlington Robinson's Letters to Edith Brower* (Harvard University Press. Cambridge, 1968), pp 119-120; printed in John William Pye, editor, *Edwin Arlington Robinson: A Bio-Bibliography* (Trinity College: Hartford, Conn., 1971), p. 5.

The original poem of six stanzas, with six verbal revisions, a subtitle in parentheses and stanzas 2, 3 heavily blacked out, was dated by Robinson "June, 1900." On June 11 he wrote Miss Brower: "I have done and am still doing a 'symbolical' Twilight Song (sic) of seventy-two lines" (p. 117).

On January 1, 1901 he told Josephine Preston Peabody: "There is something that I have not cured even by throwing away twenty-four lines, which I did with joy at [William Vaughn] Moody's suggestion. If you can improve it by tearing out two more, do so by all means. You see I tried to do something 'rather swagger' . . . and I did not quite succeed. I shall print it, I suppose, but I can't pretend that I am half-satisfied with it" (Torrence, *Selected Letters*, pp. 36-37). On January 7 he informed Edith Brower: "The four stanzas I have kept . . . do seem to me now to be pretty doubtful" (Cary, p. 135).

NORMANDY

From Edwin Arlington Robinson, *The Town Down the River* (Charles Scribner's Sons: New York, 1910), pp. 74-75.

AU REVOIR

From Edwin Arlington Robinson, *The Town Down the River* (Charles Scribner's Sons: New York, 1910), pp. 83-84.

On November 10, 1921 Robinson wrote Edith Brower: "I left out 'Au Revoir' [from *Collected Poems*] simply because no one liked it, or seemed to 'get' it— insisting upon taking it in dead earnest, when it was supposed, save in the last two lines, to be mildly humorous" (Cary, *EAR Letters*, p. 178). He wrote the poem on the occasion of Theodore Roosevelt's departure for Africa to hunt big game.

VARIATIONS OF GREEK THEMES, V

From Edwin Arlington Robinson, *Captain Craig*, revised edition (Macmillan Company: New York, 1915), pp. 174-175.

This is the only one of the twelve poems under this title which Robinson did not carry over into his *Collected Poems*. It is not, like the others, a translation from *The Greek Anthology* but an improvisation of his own.

On December 2, 1913 Robinson wrote Lilla Cabot Perry: "In making the translations — if they may be called translations — I used Mackail's *Selections*, and used them most shamelessly — I mean the

English part of them — for my knowledge of Greek was never more than Xenophontic, and now it isn't even that" (Richard Cary, editor, *Early Reception of Edwin Arlington Robinson: The First Twenty Years* [Waterville, Maine, 1974], p. 281).

BEN JONSON ENTERTAINS A MAN FROM STRATFORD

From *The Drama,* V (November 1915), 552. These seven lines which Robinson omitted from his *Collected Poems* are reprinted in Charles Beecher Hogan, *A Bibliography of Edwin Arlington Robinson* (Yale University Press: New Haven, 1936), p. 105.

NIMMO'S EYES

From *Scribner's Magazine,* LIX (April 1916), 507, 508. These two stanzas which Robinson omitted from his *Collected Poems* are reprinted in Charles Beecher Hogan, *A Bibliography of Edwin Arlington Robinson* (Yale University Press: New Haven, 1936), p. 106.

When Robinson collected the poem he retitled it "Nimmo" and revised line 1 of stanza 4, which in *Scribner's Magazine* had made direct reference: "You must remember Nimmo's eyes, I think" to "No, you will not forget such eyes, I think."

HANNIBAL BROWN

From Edwin Arlington Robinson, *Hannibal Brown* (Holling Press: Buffalo, N.Y., 1936), p. [7]; reprinted in William White, *Edwin Arlington Robinson: A Supplementary Bibliography* (Kent State University Press: Kent, Ohio, 1971), p. 136, as two couplets rather than a quatrain.

This booklet of twelve unnumbered pages published on March 14, 1936 by Howard G. Schmitt in a limited edition of twenty-five numbered copies was reproduced from an original manuscript in Schmitt's possession and illustrated by Margaret Klinke.

The date of Robinson's composition may be gauged from his letter to Lilla Cabot Perry on October 11, 1918. "To pass my time, I shall, probably, write more things in the same metre [Alcaics], of which the following is a rigid example:

> Although his wish was never to baffle us,
> Hamilton Brown was dolichocephalus:
>   His head reached half way up to heaven;
> Hamilton's hat was a number seven.

This was composed in the watches of the night, with seven thousand katydids doing their best to encourage me" (Colby College Library).

BROADWAY

From New York *Evening Sun* (November 15, 1918), 18. Misled by its absence as an entry in Hogan's *Bibliography,* Edwin S. Fussell presented "Broadway" as "An Unpublished Poem by E.A. Robinson," in *American Literature,* XXII (January 1951), 488; reprinted in William White, *Edwin Arlington Robinson: A Supplementary Bibliography* (Kent State University Press: Kent, Ohio, 1971), p. 138, with erroneous attribution to that source, as in the entry on p. 32. Correction is made in Richard Cary, "The First Publication of E.A. Robinson's Poem 'Broadway,'" *American Literature,* XLVI (March 1974), 83.

Fussell drew his text from "a fair copy of the poem, written neatly and legibly by the poet," at Harvard College Library. This differs from the *Sun* version: in stanza 1, line 5 "corybantic" for "coruscating"; stanza 1, lines 2, 4, 6 commas instead of dashes. "Irridescent" was so rendered in stanza 2, line 5 in the *Sun.* The poem appeared in "The Sun Dial," Don Marquis' daily column of humor and verse. On November 18, 1918 Robinson told Lilla Cabot Perry it was printed "without my knowledge" (Colby College Library).

THE PILGRIMS' CHORUS

From George P. Baker, *The Pilgrim Spirit* (Marshall Jones Company: Boston, 1921), pp. 77-78. This book was published on July 11, 1921 with the imposing subtitle "A Pageant in Celebration of the Tercentenary of the Landing of the Pilgrims at Plymouth, Massachusetts, December 21, 1620." It was written and produced by George Pierce Baker for the Pilgrim Tercentenary Commission of Massachusetts, and was acted and sung by the people of Plymouth, Kingston, Duxbury, and Marshfield on July 13-16, 30, August 1-3, 10-13 in the State Reservation by Plymouth Rock. In *The First Twenty Years of the MacDowell Colony* (Peterborough, N.H., 1951), pp. 6-9, Marian MacDowell gives details of the genesis, development, and performances of the pageant.

Robinson to Mrs. Louis V. Ledoux, February 2, 1921: "This reminds me that I have just got myself into trouble by agreeing to write a Pilgrims' Chorus for the coming Plymouth Pageant. If I do it at all, the only good feature of it will be the hundred dollars that I'm supposed to get for it. Cale Young Rice could do it better" (Torrence, *Selected Letters,* p. 125).

A WREATH FOR EDWIN MARKHAM

From *A Wreath for Edwin Markham: Tributes . . . on his Seventieth Birthday* (The Bookfellows: Chicago, 1922), p. 20; reprinted in Edwin Markham, *New Poems: Eighty Songs at 80* (Doubleday, Doran & Company: New York, 1932), p. ix; and in *Edwin Arlington Robinson: A Collection of His Works From the Library of Bacon Collamore* (Privately printed: Hartford, 1936), p. 31.

The book in which this quatrain first appeared was published on October 20, 1922.

TOO MUCH COFFEE

From Louis Untermeyer, editor, *Modern American Poetry: A Critical Anthology* (Harcourt, Brace and Company: New York, 1936), p. 146.

Published March 7, 1936 with twenty-five other poems by Robinson in the fifth revised edition of this anthology; reprinted in Untermeyer's *From Another World* (Harcourt, Brace and Company: New York, 1939), p. 227.

Untermeyer recounts the origin of this quatrain in the second book but comes more to the point in his "E.A.R.: A Remembrance," *Saturday Review*, XLVIII (April 10, 1965), 34: "There had been a long night of elevated discussion [at the MacDowell Colony] which turned out to be more spirituous than spiritual. The next day a postcard was slid under the lintel of the cottage in which my first wife and I were sequestered. It read: [the poem follows]. It was entitled 'Too Much Coffee'; it has never appeared in any of Robinson's works." In a letter to the present editor Untermeyer states that the verse was written in the summer of 1927.

FORTUNATUS

From Edwin Arlington Robinson, *Fortunatus* (Slide Mountain Press: Reno, 1928), pp. [9, 11, 131]. This booklet of twenty-four unnumbered pages was published by James Raye Wells in October; reprinted in William White, *Edwin Arlington Robinson; A Supplementary Bibliography* (Kent State University Press: Kent, Ohio, 1971), pp. 123-124, with an error in stanza 2, line 1; "But as you are . . . "

On August 28, 1928 Robinson wrote Wells: "I will send you a poem of six stanzas in a few days, with the understanding that I shall be free to use it elsewhere if you do not publish it before November first, and that I shall be free to print it in any future volume that I may publish" (*Edwin Arlington Robinson: A Collection of His Works From the Library of Bacon Collamore* [Privately printed: Hartford, 1936], p. 41). On September 5: "I sent the poem yesterday" (Trinity College Library). The books were ready by October 23, when Robinson declared: "I shall be glad to see the books and to sign them" (Colby College Library).

MODRED

From Edwin Arlington Robinson, *Modred: A Fragment* (Brick Row Bookshop, Inc.: New York, 1929), [vii]-xviii. This booklet of twenty-four pages was published by Edmond Byrne Hackett on February 14, 1929 in an edition of 250 copies, with this AUTHOR'S NOTE: "This deleted fragment of *Lancelot* is published now for the first time with the author's permission, and with his corrections. E.A.R."; reprinted in William White, *Edwin Arlington Robinson: A Supplementary Bibliography* (Kent State University Press: Kent, Ohio, 1971), pp. 124-129.

On January 19, 1929 Robinson wrote H.B. Collamore: "I omitted the Modred fragment from *Lancelot* because it seemed out of key with the rest of the poem — bringing in, incidentally, four new characters who did not appear again" (*Collamore*, p. 43).

"Modred" first appeared under the title "Lancelot. Canto IV" in *Three Poems By Edwin Arlington Robinson* (Cambridge, Mass., May 1928) in a pirated edition of uncertain quantity, with this NOTE: "The first two poems in this book ["Ballade of the White Ship," "In Harvard 5"] appeared in the issues of the *Harvard Advocate* of October 16 and December 11, 1891, respectively. The third is a hitherto unpublished fragment of *Lancelot* and should be inserted in the text of that poem between Cantos III and VI [*sic*]. B.F." In the Harvard copy Robinson wrote: "This book was printed without the author's permission or knowledge." On May 19, 1934 he told Collamore: "I am not ever sure of all who were implicated in the enterprise" (*Collamore*, p. 44).

For published details of the *Three Poems* printing history see Hogan's bibliography, p. 31, White's supplement, pp. 141-142, Collamore's *Collection*, pp. 42-44, and Robert C. Bates, "Edwin Arlington Robinson's *Three Poems*," *Yale University Library Gazette*, VIII (October 1933), 81-82. An undated letter by Lucius Beebe to Collamore explains that the pirated edition was published by Bradley Fiske who "originally intended to print just two, one for him and one for me, but when the printer was through there were altogether fifteen copies of the book" (Colby College Library).

After removing 500 lines from *Lancelot* Robinson said to Esther Willard Bates: "I knew all the time I was going too far. My subconscious watchdog growled" (Alice Frost Lord, "Friendly Contacts with Maine Poet Reveal Personality of Man," Lewiston *Journal Magazine Section* [October 21, 1943], A-8).

Robinson's corrections consisted of changing the title, the spelling of Mordred, inserting four commas, turning two commas into periods, one period into a colon, adjusting the typographical error "them seem" to "they seem" in stanza 4, skipping lines to create two new stanzas and closing in two others. The only verbal revision: in stanza 5, line 14 "drama" to "play, not."

PROSE

BORES

From *The Amateur* (1887), pp. 10-11; reprinted in William White, *Edwin Arlington Robinson: A Supplementary Bibliography* (Kent State University Press: Kent, Ohio, 1971), pp. 118-119. White corrects the typographical error in "deseription" and the punctuation after "Astolat" and "out," but he lists the publication of the essay as 1886 (p. 29).

This unsigned essay is one among fifteen "Published by the Class of '88 of the Gardiner High School" as a 24-page booklet. Identification of Robinson as author is established by Harriet G. Andrews, a classmate, who supplied the following explanatory footnote: "I do recall that as the close of our fourth year in High School drew near, each member of the class wrote an essay. These were published in pamphlet form which was named *The Amateur*. This took the place of a graduation, as our class was obliged to have a five year course if we graduated, owing to the School Board raising the grade of the School. As no names were published with the essays, I wrote initials under each one" (Colby College Library).

A BOOK OF VERSE THAT IS POETRY

From *Literary Review*, III (January-February 1899), 12-13; reprinted in Ellsworth Barnard, editor, *Edwin Arlington Robinson: Cen-*

tenary Essays (University of Georgia Press: Athens, 1969), pp. 72-76.

Robinson's authorship of this unsigned review is attested in his letter to Josephine Preston Peabody on August 9, 1900: "I haven't yet got over those *Enringings* in 'The Wayfarers.' The crass language I used on them in Badger's 'review' . . . . " (Barnard, pp. 77-78).

Wallace L. Anderson reprints the entire review in his "The Young Robinson as Critic and Self-Critic" in the Barnard volume. He inserts "[any]" in Robinson's second sentence but follows the *Review* uncritically in its distortions of the quotations from Miss Peabody's poems. Anderson supplies the correct word "[weeds]" instead of "needs" in stanza XXX of "The Wayfarers" but commits an error of his own in "Burden *on* the weed." Neither the *Review* nor Anderson observes the added indentation of the final line, thereby possibly missing her desire to create added emphasis.

Robinson did not relish the role of public critic. As far as is now known, he did not publish another formal book review. Around this time he wrote: "If Miss Peabody tells you that I am an untaught beast, you will tell her that I am by nature as kind hearted as a caterpillar, though I have a quaint way of smashing people's heads when I wish merely to call their attention to things of interest. A great many men and women are fond of me on account of my gentle phrasing; but as a critico-paternal altruist I am not half appreciated" (Daniel Gregory Mason, "Early Letters of Edwin Arlington Robinson: First Series," *Virginia Quarterly Review*, XIII [Winter 1937], 60-61).

THE BALM OF CUSTOM

From New York *Daily Tribune* (October 7, 1900), 8; reprinted in *New England Quarterly*, XV (December 1942), 722-723; and in William White, *Edwin Arlington Robinson: A Supplementary Bibliography* (Kent State University Press: Kent, Ohio, 1971), pp. 120-121.

On November 6, 1896 Robinson wrote: "Now I have elected McKinley, of course I feel better. I was hoping, though, that Bryan would get a larger vote, as I am coming more and more to look upon him as the greatest political figure in America snice Lincoln. To tell the truth, I thought he would be elected . . . . Things are undoubtedly better as they are, for the country is in a condition where a politic man is very necessary; but all this does not alter my opinion of Mr. Bryan as a personality" (Denham Sutcliffe, editor, *Untriangulated Stars: Letters of Edwin Arlington Robinson to Harry DeForest Smith 1890-1905* [Harvard University Press: Cambridge, 1947], p. 261).

Reporting to Josephine Preston Peabody on November 10, 1921 that his play *The Porcupine* might be produced that winter, Robinson went on: "Once this notion would have excited me, but now it leaves me 'more than usual calm.' I said that once many years ago in an editorial in the *Tribune*, and 'usual' came out *usually*. After that I wrote no more editorials . . . I couldn't get interested in anything that interested the editors. As a matter of fact, I couldn't write them anyhow, — which, I hope, was rather fortunate" (Harvard College Library).

AUTOBIOGRAPHICAL SKETCHES: HARVARD

From *Harvard College Class of 1895* (Crimson Printing Co.: Cambridge, 1915), pp. 272-273; *Harvard College Class of 1895* (University

Press: Cambridge, 1920), p. 411; *Harvard College Class of 1895* (University Press: Cambridge, 1925), p. 249.

On March 17, 1895, not two years after leaving Harvard, Robinson wrote to Harry Smith: "The other day I received a blank 'life-book' from the Secretary of the Class of '95, Harvard, for me to fill out, but I do not feel like responding. The circular that came with it says that it is sent to all past and present members of the class and to such Special Students as have had social connections with the Class — whatever that may may mean. There is also, and infinitely more to the point, a request to contribute as much as possible to the Class Fund. . . . I am in doubt as to how to reply . . . . I do not just like the notion of associating a thing of that kind with Harvard College — which is the object of almost the only patriotism I possess, notwithstanding the fact that I was there but two years, and then as a Special" (Sutcliffe, p. 216).

The information submitted by Robinson contains three errors of fact. In the 1915 report: *The Town Down the River* was published in 1910. In the 1925 report: Robinson went to England only once; the Yale degree was conferred in 1922.

MUSIC AND POETRY

From Ridgely Torrence, editor, *Selected Letters of Edwin Arlington Robinson* (Macmillan Company: New York, 1940), pp. 95-96.

This letter written on July 15, 1916 to Arthur Finley Nevin (1871-1943), brother of the American composer Ethelbert and himself a composer of operas, orchestral suites, cantatas, and masques. At this time Arthur was professor of music at the University of Kansas.

THE PETERBOROUGH IDEA

Originally published in *North American Review,* CCIV (September 1916), 448-454.

The version in this volume is the first edition of the pamphlet reprints, with the authenticating lines "Cosmus & Washburn / 605 Fifth Avenue, N.Y." in the lower righthand corner of the outside cover. According to Charles Beecher Hogan, *A Bibliography of Edwin Arlington Robinson* (New Haven, 1936), p. 51, it was "Issued early in 1917."

The frequent reprinting of this essay has created a bibliographic morass. Robinson could contribute nothing but hearsay. On September 6, 1928 he wrote from the MacDowell Colony to H.B. Collamore: "I am told here that the first reprint of *The Peterborough Idea* was printed in New York, the second in Cincinnati, and the third in Peterborough. I cannot get dates, and really know very little about them" (Trinity College Library).

Leonidas W. Payne in "The First Edition of E.A. Robinson's *The Peterborough Idea,*" *University of Texas Studies in English* (July 8, 1939), 219-231, corrects misstatements by previous bibliographers and presents in parallel columns the revisions Robinson introduced into the pamphlet version, including the new concluding paragraph of tribute to Mrs. MacDowell. On the insistence of Hermann Hagedorn, Robinson had come reluctantly to the Colony, but soon he was saying to Rollo Walter

Brown, "There's nothing I wouldn't do for Mrs. MacDowell" (*Next Door to a Poet* [New York, 1937], p. 17).

THE NEW MOVEMENT IN POETRY

From Lloyd R. Morris, editor, *The Young Idea* (Duffield & Company: New York, 1917), pp. 193-196; subtitled "An Anthology of Opinion Concerning the Spirit and Aims of Contemporary American Literature." It was published on May 9.

By way of preface Morris says: "Mr. Edward [*sic*] Arlington Robinson, author of *The Town Down the River, Captain Craig, The Man Against the Sky,* and of a comedy, *Van Zorn,* has, perhaps more than any other of our contemporary poets, sought to express an intellectual content in his verse."

MY METHODS AND MEANINGS

From Ridgely Torrence, editor, *Selected Letters of Edwin Arlington Robinson* (Macmillan Company: New York, 1940), pp. 101-104.

This leter written on July 11, 1917 to Lewis Nathaniel Chase (1873-1937), a Maine-born educator who took three degrees at Columbia University, and was at this time lecturer in contemporary poetry at the University of Wisconsin. Chase wrote books on the English drama, Emerson, Poe, Shaw, and had a hand in compiling and editing several others.

A NEW ENGLAND POET

From Boston *Evening Transcript* (March 30, 1918), III, 7; subtitled "Alanson Tucker Schumann's Unostentatious Career." Reprinted in Charles Beecher Hogan, *A Bibliography of Edwin Arlington Robinson* (Yale University Press: New Haven, 1936), pp. 176-178.

Alanson Tucker Schumann (1846-1918) lived in the house next to the Robinsons' in Gardiner. Although a generation older than Edwin, he cultivated the young man and introduced him into an elite coterie of poetry lovers and encouraged him in a low time. See Robinson's remarks on Schumann in "The First Seven Years," reprinted in this volume.

On July 31, 1924 Robinson displayed a different aspect to Laura E. Richards: "Dr. Schumann was a fairly successful and contented local doctor until poetry got him at about the age of thirty. The rest of his life was a slow debâcle, if there is such a thing, and he would have died poor, without the aid of rum (which he never 'abused') if he hadn't married some money" (Torrence, *Selected Letters*, p. 138).

ON MY "NEW ENGLAND" SONNET

From Gardiner *Journal* (February 14, 1924), [1].

This letter written on February 7, 1924 to John W. Berry, editor of the *Journal*, and published under the caption: PLEASING LETTER FROM EDWIN ARLINGTON ROBINSON REGARDING THE NEW ENGLAND SONNET. Reprinted in Charles Beecher Hogan, *A Bibliography of Edwin Arlington Robinson* (Yale University Press: New Haven, 1936), pp. 179-180, where two typographical errors and the transposition of Robinson's initials are corrected.

Robinson was nudged into this uncharacteristic self-defense by the January 25 letter of D.H. Darling to Major Berry in the *Journal* of January 31, headlined: NEW ENGLAND'S INDIGNATION AROUSED —EDWIN ARLINGTON ROBINSON'S POEM CONDEMNED. DAVID DARLING LOYAL CRITIC:

In the *Literary Digest* of Dec. 1st, appeared a reprint from the London *Outlook* of a sonnet by Edwin Arlington Robinson entitled "New England" — copy of which I enclose.

It marks a phase of New England character familiar enough and much to be deplored.

Had it first appeared at home, I could have grinned and let it pass, but I am a bit resentful at his offering it in England.

The British find rocks to heave at us without our help, and are "on the target" often enough without our giving them the range.

And I would prefer to remind the world of the rugged virtues that made New England what it is, to an exposition of her faults — especially on the hearths of her ancestors. So I have written, "New England Still."

[signed]

To see our own Mr. Robinson in the London *Outlook* on the subject of "New England" is like reading a challenge: [Robinson's "New England" and Darling's "New England Still," three outraged chauvinistic quatrains, follow].

Between publication of Darling's and Robinson's letters, editor Berry offered this one by Laura E. Richards on February 7, entitled EDWIN ARLINGTON ROBINSON'S "NEW ENGLAND" EXPLAINED: [p. 1]

I am sure that Mr. Darling will be glad as I am to learn that there has been a misapprehension as to the intention of Mr. Robinson's fine sonnet on New England. Our poet (we firmly claim him as ours, though all the English-speaking world now acclaim him) writes to me, in reply to a letter of mine:

"As for the sonnet on New England, your letter makes me wonder if you didn't read it the wrong way. It was supposed to be aimed at those who patronize New England."

This is a "good hearing," as the Scotch say, and I hasten to pass it on for the general benefit. New England people who honor and admire Mr. Robinson as poet and as man, might find it hard to accept at his hands such severe strictures as those which he seemed (on first reading) to pass on his native countryside. How infinitely pleasanter to find that he was criticizing "the other feller."

I take the liberty of enclosing another sonnet of Mr. Robinson's, one of such exquisite beauty and clarity that I am sure your readers will be glad to see it. ["The Sheaves" follows]

Puzzled as always by people's inability to comprehend meanings which to him were obvious, and possibly stung by Darling's literal-minded charges of betrayal, Robinson softened the tone of the poem when he republished it in *Dionysus in Doubt* and *Collected Poems*, substituting "Here" for "Born" in line 1, "Wonder begets" for "Intolerance tells" in line 3, "boil elsewhere" for "boil from birth" in line 4, and "We're told" for "It seems" in line 10.

MACDOWELL'S LEGACY TO ART

From New York *Times Book Review* (February 22, 1925), 2; reprinted in Charles Beecher Hogan, *A Bibliography of Edwin Arlington Robinson* (Yale University Press: New Haven, 1936), pp. 180-184.

On July 31, 1924 Robinson wrote to Edwin Markham, in part: "I am taking the liberty of writing to you as one of the judges of *The Pictorial Review's* Achievement Award for 1924 in the hope that you are sufficiently acquainted with the general nature and great importance of the Edward MacDowell Association, and the MacDowell Colony here in Peterborough, and at the same time sufficiently interested, to give the name of Mrs. Edward MacDowell, who has brought the whole thing to pass, your most serious consideration. Of course this is not to be interpreted even remotely as a request, but it is written frankly in the hope of concentrating your attention upon Mrs. MacDowell's importance" (Howard George Schmitt, "Some Robinson Letters in My Collection," *Colby Library Quarterly*, I [January 1943], 10).

A NOTE ON MYRON B. BENTON

From *Thoreau's Last Letter With a Note on His Correspondent, Myron B. Benton by Edwin Arlington Robinson* (Troutbeck Press: Amenia, N.Y., 1925), pp. 9-12.

Two hundred copies of this Troutbeck Leaflet Number Five were privately printed on April 14 for private distribution. It also contained quotations from John Burroughs and Moncure D. Conway, and "A Poem on the Death of Thoreau" by Benton. Robinson received $100 for writing this appreciation.

On June 4, 1934 Robinson wrote: "I understand that 200 copies were printed of 'Thoreau's Last Letter,' and have heard of no second printing. You could easily find out by writing to Joel Spingarn, Amenia, New York" (Carl J. Weber, editor, *Letters of Edwin Arlington Robinson to Howard George Schmitt* [Waterville, Maine 1943], p. 25).

Spingarn (1875-1939) was a professor of comparative literature at Columbia University. Troutbeck was his country home in Amenia. From 1911 to 1926 he owned and edited the Amenia *Times*, issuing from its facilities a series of *Troutbeck Leaflets*.

TRIBUTE TO THEODORE ROOSEVELT

From Frederick S. Wood, editor, *Roosevelt As We Knew Him* (John C. Winston Company: Philadelphia, 1927), pp. 391-393, published on

February 1; reprinted in William White, *Edwin Arlington Robinson: A Supplementary Bibliography* (Kent State University Press: Kent, Ohio, 1971), pp. 122-123.

Editor's preface to Robinson's remarks: "By many critics Edwin Arlington Robinson is recognized as one of our leading American poets, but it was not known until Mr. Robinson gave the following account that it was Mr. Roosevelt's practical patronage of a then unknown verse-writer, that gave him a substantial start in life."

Robinson had ample reason to laud Roosevelt, who wrote an unsolicited review of *The Children of the Night* in the *Outlook* of August 12, 1905; who persuaded Scribner's to re-issue the book in October 1905 and to open the pages of their magazine to his poems; who appointed Robinson to a position in the New York Custom House when he was on his last financial legs.

A TRIBUTE TO FRANKLIN L. SCHENCK

From Northport *Observer* (February 18, 1927), 9; reprinted in Northport *Journal* (February 18, 1927), 2; and in *Edwin Arlington Robinson, A Collection of His Works From the Library of Bacon Collamore* (Privately printed: Hartford, 1936), pp. 44-46.

Franklin L. Schenck (1856-1927), whom Hermann Hagedorn calls "a painter of creditable landscapes," was another example of the breed of eccentrics Robinson compulsively collected throughout his life. Schenck "had a handkerchief of land on Long Island, where he had a dog and some wild rabbits and raised a few chickens and vegetables which achieved a kind of transcendental existence for him" (Hagedorn, *Edwin Arlington Robinson: A Biography* [New York, 1938], pp. 322-323). He had at odd times lived with Robinson and Seth Ellis Pope in their apartment at 810 Washington Street, Brooklyn.

FRANKLIN SCHENCK (1856-1927)

From *Paintings by Franklin L. Schenck 1856:1927* (Macbeth Gallery: New York, 1928), p. [4]. This eight-page catalogue issued on February 28 for distribution to patrons of the exhibition at Macbeth Gallery, New York City, which ran until March 12.

Hagedorn (p. 323) gives no dates but declares that "Robinson, convinced that Schenck's paintings were 'the real thing,' took steps to make him known through an exhibition in the rooms of the Brooklyn Chamber of Commerce." Schenck's somber rendition of Robinson's "The Dark Hills" now hangs in Colby College Library.

INTRODUCTION TO *THE LETTERS OF THOMAS SERGEANT PERRY*

From Edwin Arlington Robinson, editor, *Selections From the Letters of Thomas Sergeant Perry* (Macmillan Company: New York, 1929), pp. 1-14; dated January 21, 1929 at the end of the essay.

Robinson's natural aversion to the academic task of editing a volume of letters was overcome by his affection for Perry, his wife Lilla Cabot, and their daughter Margaret. Robinson visited them often at their homes in Boston and at Hancock, New Hampshire, a convenient distance from Peterborough.

He decried the shortcomings of his unprofessional presentation in a letter on November 20, 1929: "The lack of an index has called down curses on my head, and with reason, as I have to admit" (William Lyon Phelps, *Autobiography With Letters* [New York, 1939], p. 697; also *Commemorative Tributes*, American Academy of Arts and Letters, [New York, 1939], pp. 15-16).

THE ARTHURIAN TRILOGY AND "RABBI BEN EZRA"

From Ridgely Torrence, editor, *Selected Letters of Edwin Arlington Robinson* (Macmillan Company: New York, 1940), p. 160.

This letter written to Helen Grace Adams on January 1, 1930. On page 190 Torrence notes: "In preparing a thesis for a Master's degree, Miss Adams had written to E.A.R., asking for a statement in regard to his 'theory of poetry and philosophy of life in general.'" Aware that what he wrote might be published, Robinson said at the close of his letter: "If your thesis is printed I should be very glad to read it."

INTRODUCTORY LETTER TO *WIND IN THE GRASS*

From Christy MacKaye, *Wind in the Grass* (Harper & Brothers: New York, 1931), p. [v]; reprinted in Edwin Osgood Grover, editor, *Annals of an Era: Percy MacKaye and the MacKaye Family 1826-1932* (Pioneer Press: Washington, D.C., 1932), p. 409. This letter was written on September 21, 1930.

Wind in the Grass is the second book of poems by Christy Lorimer MacKaye, daughter of the poet-dramatist Percy MacKaye, with whom Robinson became friendly in New York City. Of Christy's first book, *Out of Chrysalis*, Robinson wrote Percy on April 5, 1930: "I have read Christy's poems with a great deal of pleasure. She has color and warmth and something to say, and I shall look forward to her work in the future" (Grover, p. 408).

THE FIRST SEVEN YEARS

From *The Colophon*, Part Four (December 1930), unpaginated; reprinted in Elmer Adler, editor, *Breaking Into Print* (Simon and Schuster: New York, 1937), pp. 163-170; and in William White, *Edwin Arlington Robinson: A Supplementary Bibliography* (Kent State University Press: Kent, Ohio, 1971), pp. 129-135, where the print date (November), not the date of issue (December), is given.

The ornamental nine-line initial capital in *The Colophon* version was designed by Rockwell Kent, and a facsimile of the title page of Robinson's presentation copy of *The Torrent and The Night Before* to "R. Bridges, / with compliments of E.A. Robinson" accompanies the text.

FOR HARRIET MOODY'S COOK BOOK

From *The Colophon*, n.s. III (Winter 1938), [92]; reprinted in William White, *Edwin Arlington Robinson: A Supplementary Bibliography* (Kent State University Press: Kent, Ohio, 1971), pp. 136-137. The typescript copy in Colby College Library is dated 1930.

In "The Poet at the Dinner Table," *The Colophon*, n.s. III (Winter 1938), 93, Olivia H.D. Torrence states that these remarks "were written by Edwin Arlington Robinson in 1930, in response to a request from Harriet Converse Moody, widow of the poet William Vaughn Moody." She further explains that Robinson was "one of about a score of friends, all distinguished writers, whom at the suggestion of James Stephens . . . she invited, as she herself put it, 'to write some words of appreciation of the powerful appeal of epicurean food to writers of imagination . . . ' Others whom she asked were: Rabindranath Tagore, John Masefield, Padraic Colum, James Stephens, Frank Swinnerton, Vachel Lindsay, Robert Frost, Percy MacKaye, Ridgely Torrence, Leonora Speyer, Carl Sandburg, Zona Gale, Wallace Stevens, Harriet Monroe, Louis Untermeyer. Mrs. Moody's idea was that the little essays, which were to be written in any vein their authors might elect, were, grouped, to form the introduction to her book. When the manuscript was complete, Scribner's, the publishers, proved not to favor the introduction of untechnical and purely literary material. The assembled essays therefore remained unpublished."

ON THE MEANING OF LIFE

From Will Durant, editor, *On the Meaning of Life* (Ray Long & Richard R. Smith, Inc.: New York, 1932), pp. 47-49; reprinted in Ridgely Torrence, editor, *Selected Letters of Edwin Arlington Robinson* (Macmillan Company: New York, 1940), pp. 163-165. This letter, solicited as a segment for Durant's symposium, was written on September 18, 1931.

Editor's preface to Robinson's letter: "Here the vigorous rejection of mechanism by our greatest American poet:" Durant stated his intention in Chapter I of the book: "I am attempting to face a question which our generation, perhaps more than any, seems always ready to ask and never able to answer — What is the meaning or worth of human life?"

VACHEL LINDSAY

From *Elementary English Review*, IX (May 1932), 115; reprinted in Charles Beecher Hogan, *A Bibliography of Edwin Arlington Robinson* (Yale University Press: New Haven, 1936), pp. 184-185.

In the summer of 1914 Robinson wrote of Lindsay to Harriet Moody: "His chants in *Poetry* are, I fear, a bit too radical for my antiquated taste (I used to think I was modern) but I like his 'General Booth' and I believe in the man. It seems to me he has not yet found himself" (Olivia Howard Dunbar, *A House in Chicago* [Chicago,, 1947], p. 111).

THOMAS SERGEANT PERRY

From Dumas Malone, editor, *Dictionary of American Biography* (Charles Scribner's Sons: New York, 1934), XIV, 493-494; published on September 14.

Robinson wrote several times to Lilla Cabot Perry and her daughter Margaret in connection with his preparation of this essay. To Mrs. Perry (December 18, 1930: "I shall write that article on Mr. Perry and send it on to you for any changes you may like to make." On January 8, 1931: "In the meantime will you please read this enclosure for the *Dictionary of Biography* and return it as soon as you can conveniently? It is already too long (I am limited to 700 words) but you are quite free to take out anything you don't like and put in what you will. You will easily see my difficulty in working in such narrow limits, and I can only hope that the result is something like satisfactory." On January 13, 1931: "I am glad to learn that you approve of the short article on Mr. Perry, and have made the changes you suggest." On February 8, 1931: "Since you are fairly well satisfied with the the article as it is, I won't stir the matter up again unless you change your mind. The matter doesn't appear to be very important, and I'll let you see the proof anyhow." To Margaret Perry (no date): "The *Dictionary of Biography* people have made a slight change in my article on your father to the effect that he was 'associated with the *North American Review*,' where I said he was Editor. It appears that their sleuths do not find any official record of him as Editor. This isn't of much importance, perhaps, and any change would stir up a lot of machinery, for the article goes to the printer in a few days" (all quotations from unpublished letters in Colby College Library).

FOREWORD TO *THE MOUNTAIN*

From Carty Ranck, *The Mountain* (Frederick B. Ingram Productions, Inc.: Rock Island, Illinois, 1934), pp. 3-5; published on September 29.

Edwin Carty Ranck (1879-1957), another of Robinson's idiosyncratic friends, was a Kentucky journalist who attended George Pierce Baker's famous drama workshop at Harvard. Ranck published several plays, and a number of critiques and poems on Robinson, whom he considered the American poet who "should be universally known to all lovers of genuine poetry." Despite — or because of — Ranck's oddities and extremes, Robinson found that "In some strange way he has a stimulating effect on my sluggish creative faculties" (Hagedorn, p. 313).

BRIEFS

1 From *The Bookman*, V (March 1897), 7.

In the "Chronicle and Comment" section of *The Bookman*, IV (February 1897), 510, Harry Thurston Peck had written anonymously of *The Torrent and The Night Before*: "His humour is of a grim sort, and the world is not beautiful to him, but a prison-house. In the night-time there is a weeping and sorrow, and joy does not come in the morning."

On February 3 Robinson wrote: "The *Bookman* evidently takes me for a yelling pessimist, and that I must say that I am very much surprised. And the *Bookman* is not alone, either . . . . Because I don't dance on [an] illuminated hilltop and sing about the bobolinks and bumblebees, they tell me that my world is a 'prison-house, etc.'" (Denham Sutcliffe, editor, *Edwin Arlington Robinson's Letters to Harry DeForest Smith 1890-1905* [Cambridge, 1947], p. 273).

Many years later he remarked: "I was young then and it was a smart thing to say" (Nancy Evans, "Edwin Arlington Robinson," *The Bookman*, LXXV [November 1932], 680).

2 From *Edward MacDowell Memorial Association Report for the Year 1913* (Irving Press: New York, 1914), p. 9.

This letter written March 26, 1913 to Caroline B. Dow, one of the Directors of the Association.

3 From William Stanley Braithwaite, "America's Foremost Poet," Boston *Evening Transcript* (May 28, 1913), 21; subtitled "Edwin Arlington Robinson, Crowned by Roosevelt and Alfred Noyes."

Braithwaite adds immediately after Robinson's last comment: "That is more than the man has ever said before to the public."

4 From "Great Among Poets Hides in Modesty," Boston *Post* (May 30, 1913), 2.

5 From Joyce Kilmer, "Edwin Arlington Robinson Defines Poetry," New York *Times Magazine Section* (April 9, 1916), 12; reprinted as "A New Definition of Poetry," in Joyce Kilmer, *Literature in the Making* (Harper & Brothers: New York, 1917), pp. 266-[273].

6 From Herbert S. Gorman, "Edwin Arlington Robinson, and a Talk with Him," New York *Evening Sun, Books and the Book World* (January 4, 1920), 7.

7 From letter of August 1, 1920 to Louis Van Ess, "if you decide to write the paper of which you speak." *Edwin Arlington Robinson: A Collection of His Works From the Library of Bacon Collamore* (Privately printed: Hartford, 1936), p. 27.

8 From letter of April 29, 1920 to Waitman Barbe, a professor of English at West Virginia University. Cecil D. Eby, Jr., "Edwin Arlington Robinson on Higher Education," *Colby Library Quarterly*, V (September 1960), 164.

9 From letter of September 15, 1921 to the Poetry Society: *Year Book of the Poetry Society of South Carolina for 1921* (Charleston, S.C., 1921), p. 18, published October 20; reprinted in Lloyd Morris, *The Poetry of Edwin Arlington Robinson* (George H. Doran Company: New York, 1923), p. 109, where "[not]" is inserted before "always" in the last line.

10 From Theodore Maynard, "Edwin Arlington Robinson," *Catholic World*, CXV (June 1922), 374; reprinted in Theodore Maynard, *Our Best Poets* (Henry Holt & Company: New York, 1922), pp. 153-168, as "Edwin Arlington Robinson: A Humorist Who Cannot Laugh."

Maynard said: "I talked to him once about the ambiguity of meaning in the third and fourth lines of his poem 'Tact,' after I had discussed it with several friends." Robinson "was silent a moment" after the first remark, "and then added" the second.

11 From Herbert S. Gorman, *The Procession of Masks* (B.J. Brimmer Company: Boston, 1923), p. 17.

12 From letter of January 28, 1923 to Carl J. Weber in "Library Notes for E.A.R.'s Birthday," *Colby Mercury*, VI (November 1938), 213; reprinted in William Rose Benet, "Phoenix Nest," *Saturday Review of Literature*, XXVI (April 17, 1943), 54.

13 From "Young Boswell Interviews E.A. Robinson," New York *Tribune* (April 18, 1923), 13; reprinted in Young Boswell [Harold Stark], *People You Know* (Boni & Liveright: New York, 1924), pp. 221-223, published May 1.

For the book, Stark made some revisions in his own commentary but did not alter Robinson's remarks.

14 From letter, no date, to Alice Hunt Bartlett in "The Dynamics of American Poetry—III," *Poetry Review*, XV (January-February 1924), 36.

In reviewing Robinson's *Collected Poems* she exhibited confusion about "How may one express a preference in such wealth as is offered in Robinson's book. I thought the author would help me in selecting, while revealing his own preference." She was disappointed in his answer, and settled for three of his poems "regarding poets and poetry": "Oh for a poet," "Credo," "Momus."

15 From "Percy MacKaye, Poet, Honored on 50th Birthday," New York *World* (March 15, 1925), 3E; reprinted under the title "Unquestionable Genius" in *Percy MacKaye, A Symposium of his Fiftieth Birthday, 1925.* Foreword by Amy Lowell (Dartmouth Press: Hanover, N.H., 1928), p. 14, with "appears" for "seems" and minor variations in punctuation and paragraphing.

16 From Walter Tittle, "Glimpses of Interesting Americans," *Century*, CX (June 1925), 192.

17 From Robinson Jeffers, *Roan Stallion, Tamar, and Other Poems* (Boni & Liveright: New York, 1925), front cover of dust jacket.

S.S. Alberts, *A Bibliography of the Works of Robinson Jeffers* (New York, 1933), p. 24: Robinson's statement was "omitted in the rearrangement of dust-wrappers after the first printing . . . because of the customary restraint of Mr. Robinson and his distinction as a poet." Una Jeffers adds: "Mr. Robinson had written that sentence in a letter of acknowledgement and we had shown it to the publisher. But we didn't know whether permission to use this had been asked of Mr. Robinson and felt uncomfortable to see it on the dust-wrapper."

Chard Powers Smith, *Where the Light Falls: A Portrait of Edwin Arlington Robinson* (New York, 1965), p. 349: "E.A. trembled with fury when he told me of it."

Robinson explained his position to Alberts in a letter on August 7, 1931: "If the sentence you quote from the dust-jacket of *Roan Stallion* is attributed to me, it must have been taken from my letter about *Tamar*. It is barely possible that I wrote something else at the request of the publishers, and have forgotten it, but hardly probable. I have no objection to going on record as having said of Mr. Jeffers that he has 'an amazing fertility and daring,' for he certainly has both, and much more" (p. 24).

18 From Mark Van Doren, *Edwin Arlington Robinson* (Literary Guild of America: New York, 1927), pp. 30, 59.

19 From Harry Salpeter, "E.A. Robinson, Poet," New York *World* (May 15, 1927), 8M. There is no known corrected copy or typescript.

20 From M.K. Wisehart, " 'By Jove!' Said Roosevelt 'It Reads Like the Real Thing!' " *American Magazine*, CV (April 1928), 34-35, 76, 78, 80, 82, 84.

On Coan and Louis: "He [Coan] invited me to call on him if I came to New York. Later I did go to New York, and at the home of Dr. Coan I met Alfred H. Louis, who is the original of 'Captain Craig.'

So you see, if my friend Blair had not gone back for his umbrella I should never have written 'Captain Craig'!" (Carty Ranck, "Edwin Arlington Robinson," New York *Herald Tribune Magazine* [December 14, 1930], 8). Hermann Hagedorn, *Edwin Arlington Robinson: A Biography* (New York, 1938), p. 110, gives his version of this story.

Hagedorn utilized the final passage of this interview as an epigraph to his biography of Robinson, omitting the first sentence, the "and" between "abilities" and "aptitudes," substituting "everything" for "anything," and not italicizing "him."

21 From Winfield Townley Scott, "To See Robinson," *New Mexico Quarterly*, XXVI (Summer 1956), 161-178; reprinted in Winfield Townley Scott, *Exiles and Fabrications* (Garden City, N.Y., 1961), pp. 154-170.

Scott recorded these remarks at his first meeting with Robinson in August 1929 and other meetings in subsequent years.

22 From letter of October 17, 1929 in *Letters of Salutation and Felicitation Received by William Gillette on the occasion of His Farewell to the Stage in "Sherlock Holmes"* (George Tyler, 1930), p. [99].

Clayton Hamilton and Beauvais Fox compiled this booklet of sixty-one tributes, Robinson's the forty-eighth, arranged in alphabetical order, without pagination. William H. Gillette (1855-1937), theatrical star, was also author of melodramatic plays adapted from novels and foreign sources, notably *Sherlock Holmes* and *Secret Service*.

Robinson's reference is to Gillette's dramatization of *The Astounding Crime on Torrington Road*: being an account of what may be termed "The Pentecost episode" in a most audacious criminal career (New York, 1927).

23 From letter of November 18, 1929 in William Lyon Phelps, "Edwin Arlington Robinson," *Commemorative Tributes* (American Academy of Arts and Letters: New York, 1939), p. 14; reprinted in William Lyon Phelps, *Autobiography With Letters* (Oxford University Press: New York, 1939), p. 696.

Phelps was president of the Institute of Arts and Letters in 1929, the year it presented to Robinson its Gold Medal for Poetry. With characteristic reticence Robinson wrote: "At the risk of appearing a little ungracious, may I ask if anything in the nature of a formal presentation may be omitted?"

24 From Lucius Beebe, "Robinson Sees Romantic Strain In Future Verse," New York *Herald Tribune* (December 22, 1929), I, 19; subtitled "American Poet Observes 60th Birthday Today; Stresses Professionalism in Work. Discredits Self Judgment. Says Merit of Output Rests With Later Opinions."

25 From letter of January 21, 1930 in Sister Mary James Power, *Poets at Prayer* (Sheed & Ward: New York, 1938), pp. 72, 73.

Sister Power's stated purpose in her preface: "to discover the attitude toward religion of some of the generally acknowledged leaders in contemporary English and American Poetry." She placed Robinson in the category of "Seekers After God." She said of him: "Edwin Arlington Robinson, charged by some as an agnostic and a fatalist, but championed here as one, as he said himself, who could not find his way; who said that there is no man who believes nothing; who followed a flickering flame of faith which lighted up hope in a God Who guides and guards men, a God Whose ways are omnipotent, inscrutable to man, Who leads men to the conclusion that death is a beginning and not an end" (p. xix).

26 From letter of June 29, 1930 in Gerald DeWitt Sanders & John Herbert Nelson, editors, *Modern Poets of England and America* (Macmillan Company: New York, 1936), p. 387.

This letter, now in Colby College Library, reveals that the editors omitted "which explains itself" after "The Wife of Palissy"; wrote "can" instead of "could" in the last sentence.

27 From Lucius Beebe, "Dignified Faun: A Portrait of E.A.R." *Outlook*, CLV (August 27, 1930), 649.

In Conrad Aiken, "Three Meetings With Robinson," *Colby Library Quarterly, VIII* (September 1969), 346: "Unhappily I mentioned this day to Lucius Beebe who reported some of it in a magazine. Then came a sad letter from Robinson: he didn't like it to be said that he drank. What to do? I answered that I thought it was fine, and one of the best days of my life, or words to that effect. I never heard from him again. Mind you, though EAR and I never corresponded further, I *did* see him often at Lock-Ober's restaurant in Boston, and he was always cordial. I suspect he blamed Beebe more than he did me!"

28 From Carty Ranck, "Edwin Arlington Robinson," New York *Herald Tribune Magazine* (December 14, 1930), 9.

29 From *Famous Living Writers* (American Education Press: Columbus, Ohio, c1931), p. 24.

This is a set of thirty-six printed slips mounted on thin, blue cards, each with photograph and facsimile signature of the author as well as his statement on "My Favorites Among My Works."

30 From Laura E. Richards, *Stepping Westward* (D. Appleton and Company: New York, 1931), pp. 380, 382.

31 From Douglas Gilbert, "Edwin Arlington Robinson—Poet," New York *Telegram* (January 3, 1931), 13.

32 From letter, no date, to the Macmillan Company in Boston *Evening Transcript Book Section* (October 3, 1931), 8; reprinted in Charles Beecher Hogan, *A Bibliography of Edwin Arlington Robinson* (Yale University Press: New Haven, 1936), p. 184.

Robinson's letter was prefaced by these words: "Edwin Arlington Robinson is disturbed over the frequent mispronunciation of the name of the hero of his latest poem. He writes to the Macmillan Company, his publishers:"

33 From letter of December 7, 1931 to Bess Dworsky in Ridgely Torrence, editor, *Selected Letters of Edwin Arlington Robinson* (Macmillan Company: New York, 1940), pp. 165-166.

Bess Raisel Dworsky did not include this letter in her Master of Arts thesis, *Optimism and Pessimism: The Philosophical Attitudes of Edwin Arlington Robinson and Certain Similar Ideas Expressed in His Poetry and the Poetry of Robert Browning* (University of Minnesota, 1932).

Robinson began his letter: "I am naturally gratified to learn that you are writing a thesis on my poetry, but I am rather sorry to learn that you are writing about my 'philosophy' . . . "

34 From letter of January 6, 1932 to John S. Mayfield in *Vachel Lindsay by Edwin Arlington Robinson* (Privately printed for John S. Mayfield by the Fraternity Press: Washington, D.C., 1948), p. [3]; reprinted in *The Courier*, III (June 1963), 28, a publication of the Syracuse University Library Associates.

35 From letter of January 7, 1932 to Edna Davis Romig in "Tilbury Town and Camelot," *University of Colorado Studies*, XIX (June 1932), facing p. 318; reprinted in *Edwin Arlington Robinson: A Collection of His Works From the Library of Bacon Collamore* (Privately printed: Hartford, 1936), pp. 55-56; in Charles Beecher Hogan, *A Bibliography of Edwin Arlington Robinson* (Yale University Press: New Haven, 1936), pp. 185-186; and in Richard Cary, editor, *Appreciation of Edwin Arlington Robinson: 28 Interpretive Essays* (Colby College Press: Waterville, Maine, 1969), p. 37.

Robinson preceded this list with: "It is difficult to answer your letter for lack of anything very specific to say, but taking your questions in order I might say something like this:" He followed the list with: "I fear this will not be of much use to you in your talk on my work, and can only hope, with many thanks that my work will serve you better."

36 From letter, no date, to Albert O. Bassuk, in *Youth* (June 1932), 4; reprinted in New York *Times* (June 20, 1932), 17, under the headline

EINSTEIN IS TERSE IN RULE FOR SUCCESS; and in Charles Beecher Hogan, *A Bibliography of Edwin Arlington Robinson* (Yale University Press: New Haven, 1936), p. 186, with this note: "This letter was one of several written by various eminent men to Mr. Bassuk in response to his question, What is Success? The magazine in which it was printed was not formally published, and exists only in mimeograph."

Bassuk, a student at St. John's College in Brooklyn, was editor of this publication of the Young Israel of Williamsburg.

37 From Nancy Evans, "Edwin Arlington Robinson," *The Bookman,* LXXV (November 1932), 675-681.

38 From William Rose Benet, editor, *Fifty Poets: An American Auto-Anthology* (Duffield and Green: New York, 1933), p. 16.

Benet conceived the experiment of "letting the poets choose their own poems for inclusion," asking them "to add, in a brief paragraph, some of their reasons for choosing their particular poem, as well as something concerning the circumstances under which it was written" (pp. vii-viii). Robinson "answered that he really had no notion as to which of his shorter poems might have the longest life in it." Benet urged Robinson again without success. "Finally the editor suggested that he himself be allowed to choose a passage from *Tristram* which he would use while expressly stating that the selection was *not* made by Mr. Robinson . . . . The poet kindly consented, as he said he did not wish to be a dog in the manger" (p. 16). Benet entitled the passage he chose, "Tristram and Isolt of Ireland," beginning "'God knows,' he said," and ending "Of hell supplanting her" (*Collected Poems,* 1937, pp. 685-687).

39 From Karl Schriftgiesser, "An American Poet Speaks His Mind," Boston *Evening Transcript Book Section* (November 4, 1933), 1-2.

40 From letter of January 12, 1934 to Houston Martin in "With Letters from Housman," *Yale Review,* XXVI (December 1936), 294; reprinted in Ridgely Torrence, editor, *Selected Letters of Edwin Arlington Robinson* (Macmillan Company: New York, 1940), p. 174.

In his preface to this letter Martin wrote: "The late Edwin Arlington Robinson told me a short time before his death that he found a copy of the first English edition [of *A Shropshire Lad*] in a Boston bookstore in 1896. He was immediately impressed, he said, by the beauty of the poems, and he made numerous notes and allusions in his copy before passing it on to his friend, William Vaughn Moody."

41 From New York *Times* (April 6, 1935), 15.

42 From Theodore Maynard, "Edwin Arlington Robinson," *Catholic World*, CXLI (June 1935), 268, 269.

43 From Kathryn White Ryan, "Tristram," *Voices*, no. 83 (Autumn 1935), 32-36.

44 From letter, no date, to Boris Todrin in *The Room by the River* (Black Cat Press: Chicago, 1936), inside front flap of dust jacket.

The book is dedicated "To Edwin Arlington Robinson / The Man in the Room by the River."

Boris Todrin (1915-), a Fellow in residence at the MacDowell Colony in the thirties, has published at least eight volumes of poems, fiction, and social comment.

Mark Van Doren, below Robinson's blurb: "I first heard of Boris Todrin from Edwin Arlington Robinson . . . . Mr. Robinson had great confidence in the poetry which his young friend would write . . . . The result in the present case is more than a book which Mr. Robinson would have wanted to see."

45 From Carl Van Doren, "Post-War: The Literary Twenties," *Harper's*, CLXXIII (July 1936), 154, 155.

46 From Rollo Walter Brown, *Next Door to a Poet* (D. Appleton-Century Co.: New York, 1937), pp. 6, 36, 37, 38, 47, 55, 56, 62, 63, 74, 79.

Robinson's statement that reviewers had not "devoted as much as an inch to me" in his earlier years as a poet is misleading. See Richard Cary, *Early Reception of Edwin Arlington Robinson: The First Twenty Years* (Waterville, Maine, 1974).

47 From Florence Peltier, "Edwin Arlington Robinson, Himself," *Mark Twain Quarterly*, I (Summer 1937), 6, 11, 12.

48 From Daniel Gregory Mason, "Early Letters of Edwin Arlington Robinson: First Series," *Virginia Quarterly Review*, XIII (Winter 1937), 58.

49 From Hermann Hagedorn, *Edwin Arlington Robinson: A Biography* (Macmillan Company: New York, 1938), pp. 73, 89, 118, 158, 196, 209, 300, 301, 311, 370.

50 From Daniel Gregory Mason, *Music In My Time* (Macmillan Company: New York, 1938), p. 127.

51 From "E.A. Robinson: 1869-1935," *Mark Twain Quarterly,* II (Spring 1938), an Edwin Arlington Robinson Issue.

The first quotation is from John Cowper Powys, "The Big Bed," p. 2; the second from Mrs. Edward MacDowell, "Robinson at MacDowell Colony," p. 16.

52 From James S. Barstow, *My Tilbury Town* (Privately printed: New York, 1939), p. 7.

This is a literal quotation of George Burnham by Barstow.

53 From letter of December 22, 1929 to Henry E. Dunnack in C. Lennart Carlson, "Robinsoniana," *Colby Mercury,* VI (December 1939), 283.

54 From William Thomas Walsh, "Some Recollections of E.A. Robinson: Part I," *Catholic World,* CLV (August 1942), 526, 530, 531; "Part II" (September 1942), 703.

Robinson's last remark on liberalism, in "Part II," was made to Walsh in 1929.

55 From Lloyd Morris, *A Threshold in the Sun* (Harper & Brothers: New York, 1943), p. 184.

56 From Alice Frost Lord, "Friendly Contacts With Maine Poet Reveal Personality of Man," Lewiston *Journal Magazine Section* (October 23, 1943), A-8.

These remarks by Robinson were made to Esther Willard Bates.

For some of the lines removed from *Lancelot,* see *Modred: A Fragment* in the "Poems" section of this volume.

57 From Esther Willard Bates, *Edwin Arlington Robinson and His Manuscripts* (Colby College Library: Waterville, Maine, 1944), pp. 2, 5, 6, 9, 14, 19, 22, 32.

58 From Frederika Beatty, "Edwin Arlington Robinson as I Knew Him," *South Atlantic Quarterly,* XLIII (October 1944), 375, 378, 379.

See Ellsworth Barnard's version of the "hyphen from hell-hound" anecdote in *Edwin Arlington Robinson: A Critical Study* (New York, 1952), p. 276, n. 25.

59 From Leonora Cohen Rosenfield, "The Philosopher and the Poet: Morris Raphael Cohen and Edwin Arlington Robinson at the MacDowell Colony," *Palinurus,* I (April 1959), 33, 34, 35.

Rosenfield explains, "The term 'Bokardo' represents a type of syllogism in the third figure which Aristotle finds it very difficult to reduce to the first figure" (p. 33).

60 From Mabel Daniels, "Edwin Arlington Robinson: A Musical Memoir," *Radcliffe Quarterly,* XLVI (November 1962), 5-11; reprinted in *Colby Library Quarterly,* VI (June 1963), 219-233.

61 From Chard Powers Smith, *Where the Light Falls: A Portrait of Edwin Arlington Robinson* (Macmillan Company: New York, 1965), pp. 340, 351, 353.

Robinson's comment on "Mr. Flood" was made to Smith "sometime in the late twenties."

62 From Louis Untermeyer, "E.A.R.: A Remembrance," *Saturday Review,* XLVIII (April 10, 1965), 33-34.

In his last comment Robinson refers to Clement Wood, *Poets of America* (New York, 1925), p. 139: "It has bothered some commentators that so many of his New England characters have names as odd to it as they would be to old England: Flammonde, Bokardo, Briony, Argan, Ben Trovato, Penn-Raven, Umfraville, Lorraine, Gabrielle. If these are portraits of people remembered . . . "

63 From Philip Butcher, editor, *The William Stanley Braithwaite Reader* (University of Michigan Press: Ann Arbor, 1972), p. 205.

This selection is from *The Reminiscences of William S. Braithwaite,* a transcription of interviews taped for the Oral History Research Office at Columbia University on May 15, 17, and 28, 1956.

INDEX